# Where in the World Are Dick & Mary?

by

Dick Fislar

*Jessica,*
*Thanks for all you do for us! I hope you enjoy this book as much as Mary and I enjoyed our adventures. Best wishes to you always,*
*Sincerely,*
*Dick*

**DORRANCE PUBLISHING CO**
EST. 1920
PITTSBURGH, PENNSYLVANIA 15238

5-20-24

The contents of this work, including, but not limited to, the accuracy of events, people, and places depicted; opinions expressed; permission to use previously published materials included; and any advice given or actions advocated are solely the responsibility of the author, who assumes all liability for said work and indemnifies the publisher against any claims stemming from publication of the work.

All Rights Reserved
Copyright © 2022 by Dick Fislar

No part of this book may be reproduced or transmitted, downloaded, distributed, reverse engineered, or stored in or introduced into any information storage and retrieval system, in any form or by any means, including photocopying and recording, whether electronic or mechanical, now known or hereinafter invented without permission in writing from the publisher.

Dorrance Publishing Co
585 Alpha Drive
Pittsburgh, PA 15238
Visit our website at *www.dorrancebookstore.com*

ISBN 978-1-6853-7176-0
eISBN 978-1-6853-7719-9

# Contents

1. Foreword . . . . . . . . . . . . . . . . . . . . . . . . . . . . . .v
2. How We Met . . . . . . . . . . . . . . . . . . . . . . . . . . .1
3. MS *Westerdam* Inaugural . . . . . . . . . . . . . . . . . .7
4. Rome For A Weekend . . . . . . . . . . . . . . . . . . . .15
5. We Keep A Promise . . . . . . . . . . . . . . . . . . . . .25
6. September 11th . . . . . . . . . . . . . . . . . . . . . . . .31
7. The Twin Cruise . . . . . . . . . . . . . . . . . . . . . . .35
8. Carnival Cruise & Race . . . . . . . . . . . . . . . . . . .43
9. No Amount of Planning Replaces Dumb Luck . .49
10. African Safari in Kenya . . . . . . . . . . . . . . . . . . .55
11. African Safari in Tanzania . . . . . . . . . . . . . . . . .67
12. Victoria Falls, Zimbabwe . . . . . . . . . . . . . . . . .75
13. Ireland – St. Patrick's Day . . . . . . . . . . . . . . . .81
14. Grand Canyon . . . . . . . . . . . . . . . . . . . . . . . . .87
15. Budapest to Amsterdam . . . . . . . . . . . . . . . . . .97
16. Running on New Year's Eve . . . . . . . . . . . . . .105
17. Spain & Portugal . . . . . . . . . . . . . . . . . . . . . .113

18. Galapagos & Machu Picchu . . . . . . . . . . . . . .127
19. Tahiti . . . . . . . . . . . . . . . . . . . . . . . . . . . . . . .141
20. Carnival Paradise Inaugural . . . . . . . . . . . . .149
21. Magical Chiina, Yangtze River & Hong Kong .153
22. Scotland . . . . . . . . . . . . . . . . . . . . . . . . . . . .177
23. Christmas Market Cruise . . . . . . . . . . . . . . .183
24. London Paris & Normandy . . . . . . . . . . . . .189
25. Tulips & Windmills . . . . . . . . . . . . . . . . . . .197
26. Poland: Warsaw, Krakow, Auschwitz & Prague .205
27. Egypt . . . . . . . . . . . . . . . . . . . . . . . . . . . . . .219
28. Osaka, Japan . . . . . . . . . . . . . . . . . . . . . . . .233
29. Burgundy & Provence . . . . . . . . . . . . . . . . .243
30. New Years on the *Jewel of the Seas* . . . . . . . . .251
31. Lutherland . . . . . . . . . . . . . . . . . . . . . . . . . .257
32. Scandinavia & Russia . . . . . . . . . . . . . . . . .269
33. Switzerland . . . . . . . . . . . . . . . . . . . . . . . . .279
34. Antarctica . . . . . . . . . . . . . . . . . . . . . . . . . .289
35. Chasing the Northern Lights . . . . . . . . . . . .305
36. About the Author . . . . . . . . . . . . . . . . . . . .323

# Foreword

Over the years Mary and I have traveled to all fifty states, over one hundred thirty countries and soon to be, our one hundredth cruise.

When you travel that much, it is almost certain you will experience things that are not just ordinary travel experiences. In this book it is my desire to let you know about some of the exciting places we've been and what we did while we were there. What makes this book different and exciting is the unusual events we experienced along the way.

Some of our experiences were serious. All of them were quite different from what the usual tourist experiences. Each chapter tells a different story. Anyone can write about a cruise to Norway. A chapter in this book tells how Mary and Dick were dangling on a very thin cable hundreds of feet above the ocean in freezing rain and sleet below a helicopter in a hurricane in the middle of the night off the coast of Norway.

Nothing in this book would have happened without my wife Mary's input.

Mary Fislar is simply the best at what she does of anyone I know in the travel industry. Mary is very good at researching interesting destinations for us to host our friends and groups. She is even better at securing good rates and itineraries. As with everything else in my life, nothing good happens unless it includes Mary.

The policy of our travel agency has always been when people come to us as customers or clients we try to turn them into friends. Many of our closest friends first came to us as clients.

We have too many to name them all, but a few have literally traveled around the world with us. Rich and Bernadine Janik, Gary and Lynda DeMoss, Lane and Joyce Freyermuth, Fran and Theresa Prochaska, Bev Roberts and Ed DeLong stand out because they have been on our hosted trips for well over twenty years. Their devotion to us and to Picture Perfect Travel has been the reason for our success. Thank you dear friends. This book would not have been possible without you.

Daryl and Mary Reitz have traveled with us often but they proof read what I write and provide constructive advice. Without them, the book would look much different. My favorite sister-in-law, Marcy Bell is always helpful and travels with us often. Thank you Daryl, Mary and Marcy. I don't know what I'd do without you.

Without a computer guru a book like this just doesn't happen. Bob Swanson is that guru with both books I've written. Thank you for all the hours you've spent working on my books, I appreciate everything you've done, thank you!

As you read this book I hope you will enjoy the read as much as Mary and I have enjoyed the travels that have allowed us to create this book.

Thank you, family, friends, clients and runners. Mary and I appreciate all of you more than you know. We look forward to sharing more adventures as we all travel the world together.

Sincerely

Dick Fislar

# How We Met

I remember the day like it was yesterday but it was over forty years ago. It was a beautiful Sunday, August 3rd. The temp was over eighty degrees, not a cloud in the sky. Just a perfect day for beaching it at my favorite lake in Central Illinois.

Having been there from mid-morning, at two P.M. I decided it was time to shower the sand off, dress and head for home. This was also a perfect day for driving my 1973 bright red Pontiac Grandville Convertible with the top down.

There was a strikingly beautiful young lady I had noticed. She was with another gentleman and a young child about two years of age. She and I arrived at the beach shower to remove the sand at the same time and we shared a pleasant conversation. She didn't have wedding rings and I asked if she was in a serious relationship. She said, "no". It just seemed like we were an instant connection, so being a little bold I asked for her phone number.

I didn't have anything to write down the number but I assured her I could remember it. She told me the number, which I still remember to this day. She probably thought she would never hear from me. A few days later I called. We had a friendly chat and decided to go for dinner the next weekend at a great steakhouse, called The Boars Head. The New York strips, tossed salad and cheesecake were wonderful and so is the friendship and marriage that has endured over these forty years.

For several years I commuted on weekends between Peoria and the Quad Cities. Finally, I was in a position to move to the Quad Cities, figuring my working days were behind me and I didn't need another job!

Mary was managing a travel agency. One day she said to me, "I'd really like to have my own business." I was able to finance the opening expenses and had the business background while she had the necessary travel background.

We opened Picture Perfect Travel in Rock Island August 1, 1991. As I remember we made our first sale on

August 3rd. Over these past thirty years we've had the most wonderful work experience you can imagine. Someone, I don't remember who, once said, "If you like what you do, for a living, no day will seem like work."

In our thirty years in the travel business, we specialized in hosting groups to exotic destinations around the world. We developed an expertise in the cruise industry that not many in the industry could match that we know of. We always tried to make our clients our friends. They have been very faithful to our business. Some have followed us completely around the world as well as from the Arctic to the Antarctic.

Shortly after we opened the business we traveled to Antigua and we married on August 3rd at two P.M. You've probably noticed August 3rd has been a very important day in our lives. Every August 3rd we've traveled someplace in the United States for our anniversary and enjoy our anniversary dinner of New York strips, tossed salad and cheesecake. We've done some amazing things for our anniversary. In later chapters we'll talk about some of them such as hiking the Grand Canyon on our anniversary.

Over the years, we have been fortunate to visit all fifty states, over one hundred and thirty of the one hundred ninety countries of the world, and to cruise on almost one hundred cruises. It has been a wonderful way to make a living!

We were recognized by our peers as knowledgeable professionals in the travel business. I was elected to the Board of Directors of Mast Travel Network. Mast is one of the largest travel consortiums in the United States. One year later I was named the Chairman of the Board and CEO of Mast, where I remained for the next five years. Mary was a gracious first lady and was instrumental in bonding travel agencies and travel suppliers together in a spirit of friendship and cooperation no other consortium has ever matched.

Throughout the following chapters we'll share with you some very exciting adventures we've experienced in our global travels. We've had some very happy, some very sad, and yes, even a few life-threatening adventures. We hope you will enjoy our stories and perhaps whet your appetite to travel, or travel vicariously through our exciting experiences.

What happened to the Pontiac Grandville Convertible? I drove it for a while and stored it for over twenty years. I sold the house where it was stored and had actually forgotten it was there. I received a call from the new owner and he asked that I move this, "piece of junk" from his home.

Mary took one look at the car and declared it would never run. Previous renters had used it as a work bench and paint bench. To be honest I wondered if it would start but I had to move it from Peoria to the Quad Cities, well over a hundred miles.

I had brought a new battery and five gallons of fresh gas. I installed the battery and put the gas in the tank. To both of our surprise it started on the first try!

Mary was to follow in our car, and I would drive BIG RED. We were fifteen miles into the drive and the muffler fell off. It sounded like a truck but we forged ahead. A couple miles further, the thermostat stuck and the engine overheated.

We were almost to Princeville, Illinois and I managed to get it to an auto repair shop. It was late at night by this time so we left the keys, the car and a note. It was repaired and a few days later we drove it back to Rock Island in the Quad Cities where I stored it for another five years.

When we married and bought a house, I moved BIG RED to our home and decided to restore BIG RED. He is now one of the most beautiful cars in the Quad Cities and runs like a Swiss watch after having a new top, new paint, new upholstery, and the engine completely rebuilt. Every time we drive BIG RED, I reflect on the day we met and how far we've traveled on the road of life together.

*Big Red*

# MS Westerdam Inaugural

Being a Travel Agent does have some pretty nice perks from time to time. One perk is when a new cruise ship is built the cruise line will invite certain agents from Travel Agencies with a potential to sell that ship on what they call an inaugural cruise.

Inaugural cruises are really exciting. When you're invited it's a great honor because you will be sailing on a new ship. The crew on a new ship is selected from the best employees in the company. They are usually the best of the best. The inaugural sailing always has the highest level executives in the company on board with you. The CEO, the President, and the Board of Directors are usually all present, and we get to rub elbows, socialize and get to know them.

The best part is the cruise, the food and the drinks are all complimentary. Usually, your only cost is to get you to and from home and the ship. The cruise line always serves their finest menu items and there is never a limit to what or how many alcoholic or soft drinks you consume. They also bring their best entertainment for these events. Travel Agents are almost always given great cabin assignments.

Holland America Line Invited Mary and me to the inaugural for their ship the MS *Westerdam*. What was unusual for this inaugural was not only a new ship but we would be the very first passengers to experience their new private island, Half Moon Cay!

We boarded in Ft. Lauderdale about one P.M. on a Friday afternoon. How important we felt when they assigned cabin stewards to personally escort us to our cabin and our cabin was a balcony cabin, mid ship on a high deck.

Friday afternoon and the entire day Saturday we were at sea. Waves were calm, food, drinks and entertainment top notch. Sunday morning, we arrived at Half Moon Cay and the weather was beautiful.

Because Half Moon Cay was still being developed, they did not have a pier built yet to dock the ship so we had to tender to the island on small boats that would hold about forty or fifty passengers. We were lucky. We caught an early tender to the island arriving about 11:00 A.M. The ship was scheduled to leave at 3:00 P.M., so we had plenty of time for lunch and to explore the island.

There were only two small buildings. A large outdoor bar had only a thatched roof. One was a kitchen where they prepared food. The other was a gift shop that had a small bathroom. We had a delightful shore lunch. We dined outdoors on picnic tables under a beautiful blue sky.

After lunch, about 1:00 P.M., I suggested to Mary that we walk the beach. As we walked, we looked out to the ship anchored off shore. Behind the ship it looked like a black wall, as high and wide as we could see, that was moving rapidly toward the ship and directly toward us! Within minutes we could not even see the ship because the sky was so black. We were being drenched in a violent Caribbean thunderstorm.

There were almost two thousand people on the island with no shelter or places to keep dry. The cruise line kept providing drinks for those that wanted them. It surprised us because everyone was soaking wet and very cold. We couldn't imagine drinking under those conditions but many people were really drinking heavily!

It is hard to describe what it's like to be caught in a Caribbean thunderstorm without shelter. The rain came in sheets and lightning and thunder flashed and boomed! People huddled together and tried to find trees and bushes to shelter behind. Three o'clock came and went but there was no way off the island because waves in the ocean were so large our small tender boats were not safe to get people back to the ship.

Darkness closed in and the storm continued. It was decided we had to try the tender boats to return to the ship around five P.M. They somehow devised a lottery system to draw lots for an orderly boarding on the tender boats. We drew one of the last tenders to leave the island.

When we finally were allowed to board the tender boat, it was close to seven P.M. They had done their best to bail as much water out of the tender before we boarded but it was still ankle deep. It should be noted the tender boats were enclosed but had a couple sun roof holes in the top. We were told these boats were supposed to be unsinkable. I thought, right, so was the *Titanic*!

When we left the protected inlet and entered the ocean itself, we found ourselves in waves of eighteen to twenty feet high. We would settle into the bottom of the swells and the waves would crash over the top and we had water up to our knees in short order. Those that had continued to drink the entire day became sick at their stomach and were throwing up almost at once because of the violent turbulence.

Several people were in a panic and truly unstable during this very rough ride. Mary and I were not sick because we didn't drink like others had. We tried to calm people's fears even though we were not the most comfortable with this situation either. I do believe we made a difference to several of the younger people.

The ship had attached a set of stairs down the side of the ship with a small platform to step on as you left the tender boat. The problem was, with eighteen to twenty foot waves the tender could not get close enough to attach itself to the steps. We made three unsuccessful attempts. On the fourth try they changed drivers and we were able to tie onto the steps and stabilize the tender to the stairs. Even though we were now attached to the stairs, the ship, the stairs and the tender were being tossed violently.

Mary is always very tentative about moving when her footing is unstable. I told her, "When they tell you to move, you need to do it!" I really didn't need to worry about this because two big burly men were on the platform and each would take you by the arms, pick you up and simply deposit you from the boat onto the platform. When we found ourselves on the platform, we were still almost waist deep in water.

When we reached the top of the stairs and entered the ship, we were in the atrium area. Several crew members had large tubs of warm towels and they wrapped each of us in them!

There is no way to describe the feeling of relief we experienced for being safe and warm after so many hours. We went directly to our cabin for a warm shower and change of clothes.

Our dinner reservations were for six P.M. Of course we had missed them. Back then there was no such thing as anytime dining; you had to have dinner at your assigned times or go to the Lido lounge for the buffet.

I told Mary we could still make the late dining. She was a little worried because we had early dining reservations. We decided as sick as most people were, they would accept anyone that could make it to the dining room. We relaxed and had a lovely dinner and a bottle of wine.

The ship was late getting back to Ft. Lauderdale on Monday. We had a late flight and had no problems returning home. There was no doubt this was a most unusual and memorable inaugural cruise aboard the MS *Westerdam*. Every Holland America person had been professional and took very good care of everyone. Needless to say, we were glad to be safe at home.

A few years passed and we had the opportunity to return to Half Moon Cay. It's amazing what several million dollars and several years making improvements can do for these private islands owned by cruise lines.

Our ship was able to dock at a real pier. No tender rides this time. The weather was bright sunshine and one of the most perfect days you could have at sea. Several new buildings were constructed. I had heard about a nice little Bahamian Chapel recently constructed. I told Mary this was something we should not miss seeing. It was nestled among the foliage, complete with gorgeous purple bougainvillea flowers complimenting its peaceful setting.

This little chapel was small but it had a warm, comfortable, peaceful, intimate and loving feeling to it. We were alone, and I surprised Mary when I said to her, "Will you marry me?" She did me the favor of saying, "Yes." We've had many happy years together and of course many quite special feelings about Half Moon Cay.

***The Chapel on Half Moon Cay***

# Rome for the Weekend

Did you ever wake up in the morning and say to yourself, "I need to get away this weekend?" Of course, we all have. This happened to us a while ago. We went to the office and found a great air fare and some really good hotel prices for a weekend trip to Rome, Italy.

We called a couple who are good friends and told them what we were thinking of doing and they said, "Let's do it!" This was on a Monday and we left out of Chicago Thursday evening on a direct flight to Rome. We arrived in Rome very early morning on Friday their time.

The trip to the hotel was about an hour and a half so we arrived mid-morning. We were scheduled to leave Monday morning early. Since we had so little time from Friday noon till Monday morning we had to make the most of our time.

Even though we were dead tired from the overnight flight we decided to see as much as we possibly could.

The Concierge was very helpful. He booked us tours for Friday afternoon to the Catacombs, Saturday he arranged a VIP tour of the Sistine Chapel and Saturday afternoon a City Tour that included the Colosseum.

What really excited Mary and me was when he told us the Rome Marathon was Sunday morning. Almost 50,000 runners would participate! He tried to help us get registered to run the 5K race that was also a part of the Marathon events. Because of language and being so close to the event we were not successful. We were disappointed but we had lots to do with our three tours.

We did the Catacombs tour Friday and it was very interesting. By the time we returned to the hotel it was late enough we could check in and freshen up before dinner. By this time we had been up about thirty hours without sleep!

The concierge suggested a very nice restaurant close to the American Embassy. It was a classy restaurant with a completely glass enclosed serving area on the sidewalk. The walls, ceiling and even the doors were glass. This held about ten or twelve people. What a great atmosphere and the food turned out to be excellent.

Just as we were finishing our wine and desert the entertainment arrived. An accordion, a violin and a tambourine. The accordion man looked at me and made motions like he wanted me to video their act. So I did. These people were very high energy. They bounced all over from table to table of course singing in Italian. The locals were almost rolling in the aisles and all we could understand were words such as, airplane, baseball, and Americano. I know we were being made fun of but I was never able to show my video to anyone at home that could understand what he said. At any rate, the locals loved it. In truth, we did too.

It was a short night for sleeping. We had to be up early for our VIP tour of the Sistine Chapel. If you're going to visit the Sistine Chapel don't stand in the general admission line. You could have a birthday before you get inside. By all means pay for a tour that has special access through a private group entrance at a scheduled time. Regardless of your faith the Sistine Chapel is a must see attraction in Rome.

We returned to the hotel just in time to catch the city tour. This was interesting but with the Marathon being the next morning several streets were closed. We did see the Colosseum from the outside and many of the interesting historical sites and returned to the hotel again in time to freshen up for dinner.

Dinner Saturday evening was also a very nice restaurant where we had some great pizza. The waiter asked if we wanted some bread and oil while we waited. Of course we did and he kept it coming. Ron said he'd pay the bill so I calculated our part and gave him money to pay. As we walked down the street I asked, "Did I give you enough for our part of the bill?" He replied, "Almost". I actually thought I had given way more than necessary. We looked at the bill and you would not believe what we were charged for the bread! We found out at the hotel later that is a favorite way to raise a tourist's bill in Italy. Now we know.

Our friends were Catholic and wanted to go to Mass early at a church close to the hotel Sunday morning. We really wanted to go see the start of the Marathon. The decision was made to split up. They go to mass and we go to the Marathon and then on Sunday afternoon all of us would go to St. Peters.

The marathon started right next to the Colosseum and that was only about a mile from our hotel. We decided to put on our running clothes and we would run to the starting area. To many people that might be something strange to do. Mary and I have been running together for almost as long as we've known each other and a favorite thing for us is to run in places we travel. We've enjoyed doing that all over the world and we've seen things most tourists never have the privilege to see.

We arrived early enough to see great pre-marathon activities complete with Roman soldiers, Gladiators and much more. It was one of the most exciting things we'd ever seen prior to the start of a marathon or major race.

Not being registered we knew we could not officially run the event. We did want to get some feel of the excitement of running with 50,000 runners. We decided to stand on a street corner a couple blocks down the course and wait till the fastest runners went by and then just blend in and run a couple miles and get out.

The gun went off. The elite runners led off followed by this massive group of runners. Music playing, excitement at a high level.

As we stood on the curb looking for a good spot to join in, a fellow rushed up to Mary and handed her a very large flag on a very long pole! The flag had the outline of the United States with soccer balls placed on the flag in places where major cities would be. Chicago, Detroit, New York, among others. The flag however was in the colors of Italy. He never said a word, he gave Mary the flag and took off running!

*Rome Marathon Flag*

We were absolutely shocked! Mary looked at me and really didn't know what to say. Finally she said, "What are we going to do with this?" I said, "I don't know but maybe we can run with it for a while." Mary said, "It's way too big for me to carry, you'll have to carry it."

This flag was on about a five foot pole and the flag itself was four or five feet wide by two or three feet in height. It was a hard thing to run and carry the flag. I think that was why he wanted to get rid of it.

We started running with the flag and being the ham that I am, I started to wave it around. The spectators on the sidewalks cheered and yelled at the top of their voices as we passed them. Mary and I got so caught up with running, waving the flag and working the crowd that it was not until we passed the thirteen mile marker that we realized we could be in trouble. We didn't have the foggiest notion where we were!

Fortunately for us I had taken a business card from the hotel. It had the address on it. We pulled over to the curb and exited the race. There was a policeman nearby. He spoke no English and my Spanish didn't help too much in Italy. The policeman found a person that spoke broken English and that person gave us a general direction and sent us in the direction of the Colosseum. Once we found the Colosseum we were able to find our way back to our hotel. Of course, we were still clutching the flag!

Our friends were worried because we were so late getting back but they had a great laugh about our experience. There was just enough time for us to shower and head to St. Peters.

St. Peters Basilica is one of the most impressive structures we've ever experienced. We spent hours exploring the artwork, sculptures and statues. There is an elevator that will take you up several stories and you can walk completely around outside. However, the very best view of Rome possible is from the very very top of the dome. You reach this by taking a stairwell that is only shoulder width that extends upwards for, if my memory serves correct, three hundred forty steps. Keep in mind Mary and I had already run close to fifteen or sixteen miles. Those stairs were brutal!

Every fifty or sixty steps was a small opening where we could get a little fresh air. When we reached the top, quite exhausted, the most amazing view of Rome was before us. It was quite worth the effort.

We wondered about how to get down because the way up was far too narrow for anyone to pass. It turned out there was a corresponding set of steps only for going down.

When we got down we were just in time to see a wedding take place. This drew quite a large crowd and just seemed to finish the day at St. Peters on a very high note.

Dinner that night was just a quick sandwich at our hotel because we had a very early taxi to take us back to the airport. We had a 9:00 A.M. flight. We needed to be at the airport three hours prior to the flight and it was an hour and a half from the hotel to the airport. We asked to be picked up at 4:00 A.M.!

When the taxi arrived it was pouring rain and so dark you could barely see. The other three fit into the back seat and I was in the front with the driver. Never have we had a more thrilling drive. Our driver did not speak English, at least that we knew, but I'm sure he knew we were scared to death. He drove as fast as he could possibly go in a driving storm. We almost kissed the ground when we arrived at the airport.

Of course we still had the flag. I told Mary we had to take the flag off the pole and leave it. Never did I think we could get it on the plane with that long pole. She said, "No, the flag came on the pole it needs to stay on the pole."

The flag came home on its pole. I believe the flag had something to do with an international Italian soccer tour of the United States and we were able to sweet talk the flight attendants to let us put it under the seats. Yes, we still have the flag. I've attached a picture in this chapter for you to see!

We were in Rome only seventy-two hours. I believe we saw more and did more in that time than most people do in a week. It was an exciting and memorable time.

# We Keep A Promise

Mary has been an important member of Rotary for many years. In those years we have formed many friendships as well as business relationships with members.

One member came to us to purchase a cruise vacation. Over the years he and his wife purchased their travel from us as well as traveling with Mary and me in our hosted groups. Even though they were quite a bit older than us we became close friends.

His wife called and told us he had experienced a very serious medical issue and had spent several days in the hospital. She advised us he was currently in a long term care facility in critical care.

We went to visit every day for a week or so and on one visit his daughter asked to speak to me outside in the hallway. She told me she had met with his Doctor earlier in the day and was told he had at best a day or two to live.

When we left that evening we told him that when he became well again we'd take him on another cruise. We visited with him for a period of several weeks and each night we left him with the same message. "When you're well we'll take you on another cruise."

Slowly he began to rally. It was almost a medical miracle but Mary and I visited every day and continued to give him the same message when we left.

He recovered to the point where he was able to return to his home!

Mary and I agreed we had made a promise and we had to keep it! We found a seven night cruise from Miami that included Belize, Honduras, Costa Maya and Cozumel, returning to Miami. They, of course, were excited that we were keeping our promise to take them on a cruise.

Our flight was at 6:00 A.M. They lived only ten minutes from the airport but because they needed so much assistance we decided to pick them up at their home at 3:30 A.M. Very early for everyone but they were ready when we arrived. Boy, were they ready!

When they opened the door for us we could see a large pile of luggage! I counted thirteen pieces. I asked her, "How many of these are we taking?" She said, "All of them."

They were not all large pieces but we had to account for all of them plus Mary and I each had a carry-on and a checked piece. Total of seventeen pieces to keep track of and move through airports, taxi cabs, hotels and cruise ships.

We had to pay extra luggage fees for nine pieces in both directions. Also, we hired porters every chance we needed to move all those pieces. Their cabin would not hold all of them so we had to store some on their balcony as well as a few in our cabin.

She could walk but very slowly. I had to push him in a wheelchair to dinner, the shows, shops on the ship and to the outdoor decks. All this was fine with Mary and me. We had decided long ago this cruise was not for us to have fun, it was to keep a promise we made to our very sick friend.

For the first five days all went well. We all enjoyed the food, the shows, the open sun decks. The women certainly enjoyed the many shops and the shopping they took part in. They were not able to get off in ports for shore excursions and we had been to all of them before so we did not do anything either. We did take them off the ship a couple of times to shop in the small shops surrounding the ship's docking area. That was difficult because of her physical limitations and his being confined to a wheelchair but we all had fun in the shops.

About the fifth day he became ill and we were off to the ship's Doctor. With prescribed medicine they had on board he was able to continue to go to shows and meals. We did learn a hard lesson about travel documents, however.

The Doctor did suggest that perhaps we should send him home from the port of call the next day. It would be necessary for all of us to disembark in Cozumel and fly home from there. That was not possible in this case.

In the United States you can take a cruise without a passport under certain conditions. You can do this as long as the cruise leaves and returns to the same port. All you need for males is a birth certificate issued by a government with an official seal attached and a government issued photo ID. In the case of women that are or have been married they must also show marriage licenses to show how they moved from their birth name to the name they currently have. Keep in mind hospital birth certificates are just souvenirs from the hospital and are not an official document so they are not valid for travel.

Mary and I had our passports but there was no way to fly or enter the country for our friends with their documents. We all stayed on board to the end of the cruise and we did have a good time.

On the day we disembarked the ship we had a late afternoon flight. We hired two porters to collect our seventeen pieces of luggage. They took us to the taxi stand. It took quite a while to find a transfer to the airport because of the seventeen pieces of luggage. When we arrived at the check-in counter of the airline our friend's wife said to me, "Where is my red suitcase?"

I said, very calmly, "It has to be here because we had all seventeen pieces."

She replied, "I had one more piece today because I bought so many souvenirs."

Of course, we had left her red suitcase in the terminal after we had disembarked. I called the cruise line right away but they told me it takes twenty-four to forty-eight hours to locate luggage left at the terminal. After we returned home, I did locate their red suitcase and had it shipped to them.

Our friend lived a couple more years after the cruise. We were honored to be invited to celebrate his 90th birthday that was only open to family and to us. At that party he told us and his family, the only reason he survived the long term care illness was each day he dreamed of going on the cruise we had promised him each night as we were leaving.

Keeping our promise was not easy to do. However, knowing we helped two elderly friends have such a good time in their twilight years made it all worthwhile. We will never forget them and we feel very good for knowing them and having had them as our good friends.

# September 11th

Everybody knows where they were on September 11, 2001. We certainly remember. We were on a cruise ship in the Pacific Ocean off the coast of the big island of Hawaii.

We had a small group on board the SS. *Independence*, a ship owned by American Hawaii Cruise Line. We had sailed from Maui on Saturday, September 8th. We had made two stops on the Big Island of Hawaii. Because of the nine hour time difference, it was the middle of the night when Mary's sister knocked on our cabin door and told us what was happening in New York, Washington D.C., and Pennsylvania.

The *Independence* was an older ship and did not have televisions in the cabins. The only TVs were in the public areas of the ship. We quickly dressed and went to the lounge. The lounge filled quickly as the news spread. Everyone watched in disbelief.

Our Captain announced the ports were being closed for security reasons and we would be spending days at sea. Two of our group were veterans and had come with us mostly because the stop in Oahu would give them the chance to see Pearl Harbor and go to the Arizona Memorial.

We were able to dock in Oahu, but Pearl Harbor and the Arizona Memorial were closed. Our veteran friends were truly disappointed but there was nothing that could be done for them.

Twenty years ago cell phones were not what they are today. When we were ashore in Oahu we contacted American Airlines for instructions because flights had been grounded since Tuesday. Everyone in the group except Marcy, Mary and me were on American flying back to Chicago. The three of us were on American Trans Air flying back to Milwaukee.

Our ship docked Saturday morning and we all transferred to the airport. Mary and I went with our group to the American ticket counter. American advised they were severely backlogged and could not get our people out until Monday at the earliest. They provided all of them two nights' hotel and an allowance for food.

American Trans Air flight was on schedule because they only flew to Hawaii a couple times a week and they had no backlogged passengers. Our flight left late evening on Saturday and we arrived back in Milwaukee as scheduled on Sunday with no delays.

We were grateful to be back in the office on Monday because we had clients that were stranded in various places and we needed to be there to help them.

The rest of our group arrived home Tuesday morning. All worked out for our people for the return. However, the veteran that had most wanted to see Pearl Harbor was never able to return. He passed away without fulfilling his greatest dream. We think of him often.

It should be noted that the American Hawaii Cruise Line was never able to recover from the canceled cruises because airlines were not flying and people were truly afraid to board a flight. American Hawaii Cruise Line filed for bankruptcy and did not survive 9/11. We all know those couple days changed the world and each of our lives forever.

# The Twin Cruise

Princess Cruise Lines would be launching a new ship called, the *Dawn Princess*. It was an exact duplicate of their existing ship, the *Sun Princess*, except for the interior decorations. They were identical twins.

They decided to launch a marketing plan to promote the arrival of the *Dawn Princess* where they would select fifty sets of identical twins from across the United States and Canada to participate in Miami with the naming ceremonies prior to the ship sailing on its inaugural. The fifty sets of identical twins selected would receive a free cruise on the inaugural cruise from Miami, through the Panama Canal to Acapulco.

The rules were very specific. The twins must be nominated by someone. They could not nominate themselves. They must be identical, not fraternal. The twins must have done something significant with their lives. The person nominating them must provide 8 x 10 inch color photos of each twin along with their nominating essay of 500 words or less.

It was an overwhelming success. Over three thousand sets of identical twins were nominated from across the United States and Canada. Accepted were cancer research scientists, Holocaust survivors, the original double mint twins, classical concert musicians, just to name a few. Their ages ranged from eight to over ninety years of age.

Mary and Marcy had spent years through their church adopting elderly women and helping them through the difficult final years of their lives. They would purchase groceries, pay bills these women could not pay on their own such as telephone, utilities and cable, and sometimes even help pay their rent. They used their own money. When needed, the girls would drive these elderly women to Doctor and hospital visits. They were generous with their time and money to ensure comfortable lives for women in their declining years.

I had not told the girls what I was doing for them until it was necessary to go to a professional photographer to get their pictures taken. Princess wanted pictures of them dressed in matching clothes. I finished the nominating essay and sent it to Princess being certain to follow the rules exactly.

Several weeks passed. It was long enough that we had almost forgotten and most certainly did not feel we had been successful. In my nominating essay I had to leave a telephone contact number. We left our office telephone number. The Vice President of marketing called and gave us the good news that Mary and Marcy had been selected as one of the fifty sets of twins!

That set off a frenzy of shopping. Princess wanted the selected twins to dress as much alike as possible during the naming ceremonies as well as while on this twelve day cruise. Mary and Marcy had never dressed alike on purpose, so they had a good time buying clothes together.

Mary and Marcy were rewarded with a free twelve day cruise. What, you may ask, did Dick get for writing the nominating essay? I received a set of glass bookends etched with a picture of the *Dawn Princess*.

Of course I wanted to join Mary on the cruise. I had to pay a single supplement for my cabin even though

Mary would join me in the cabin. In other words, I paid twice the price of a single person for the cabin. That was a very expensive essay and bookend! It was very much worth it however.

We received a call from clients of ours that wanted to book this very same cruise. Mary made the booking but did not want to tell them about what she was doing as a twin. It turned out Rich and Bernadine have been some of our most loyal and faithful clients. It is more important they have been some of our very best friends for years.

I flew to Miami from Chicago on the day of the cruise. This is never a good idea but it did work out for me since it was a direct flight. I didn't need to go early because Mary and Marcy were busy with official duties until they boarded the ship. We met just as I was checking in for the cruise. I arrived about 2:00 P.M. and the ship sailed at 5:00 P.M.

This itinerary had several ports of call we had never experienced. We had two nights at sea and a day in Grand Cayman before we stopped in Cartagena, Columbia. The shopping around the pier was excellent.

Pricing was reasonable and the silk products seemed to be excellent quality. What we had never experienced in cruise ports before was very heavy military security with AK-47 type weapons. Of course we had seen security in other ports but absolutely nothing compared to Cartagena.

The San Blas islands were very interesting. Mary and I had a balcony cabin and we had the door open to the balcony. We heard voices just outside chanting, "Money, money, money, money!" Young children in very old row boats were asking passengers to throw money to them. When passengers would throw bills or coin the children would dive down under water to retrieve the money.

The Captain kept asking the passengers not to throw money because the ship's engines caused currents that could drown these children if they were caught in them. We had made it to the top deck by then and could see the ship was surrounded by numerous boats with these small children. The Captain's message was ignored by the passengers until we began boarding the tenders to go ashore. Fortunately no children were harmed.

The three islands were called, San Blas A, San Blas B and San Blas C. Natives had their trinkets spread out for sale and were very friendly. Princess had not provided transportation between the islands. Only to and from island A. To see the other two you had to hire a local to row you between those islands. I found an older gentleman to row us in a dugout canoe between islands. His fee was two dollars for Marcy, Mary and me. With the four of us in the canoe, water was only inches from coming over the top.

Our person looked to be quite old. Mary was being friendly and was talking a blue streak to him as he paddled. He was nodding his head vigorously and smiling from ear to ear as he paddled us furiously from island to island. It turned out he only knew two words in English, they were, "Two dollars."

When we returned to island A, Mary found the first lady she had talked to and purchased a couple Molas. Molas are quilted squares that can be used as pillows, pot holders or handling hot items or just for decoration.

The next day we do a full transit of the Panama Canal. We got up early and found chairs on the top deck facing forward. We enter locks at sea level that are much taller than our ship. The doors close behind us and we begin our rise to the level of the canal. The transit of the canal is a peaceful experience. The ship moves slowly and passes other ships moving in the opposite direction also moving slowly. Some areas are very narrow, others much wider. It is very quiet. You hear the birds chirping and animals on shore. The continental divide is only twenty feet tall. We found this canal transit a most calming and serene experience. We kept our places for the entire transit!

Costa Rica was our last port of call. We did a shore excursion through the rain forest and to a coffee plantation that we thought was very interesting.

The next two days were at sea enjoying the amenities of the *Dawn Princess*. We disembark in Acapulco and proceed directly to the airport. Our flight home took us through Mexico City to Chicago where I had left our car.

We met so many amazing sets of twins that had done outstanding things with their lives. Meeting these people, hearing their stories and knowing that Mary and Marcy were a part of them was worth as much or more than the cruise itself. It was truly a very rewarding experience. Thank you Mary and Marcy!

# Carnival Cruise & Race

Like I mentioned earlier Mary and I have hosted groups of various interests to exotic as well as domestic destinations. Two of our favorite things to do with our time are running and cruising.

We decided to promote a cruise to our running friends. Carnival Cruise Lines had a great seven night cruise from Miami sailing to Jamaica, Grand Cayman, San Juan and Cozumel. It was a great itinerary and was a very good price for a seven night cruise. Runners always appreciate a good value and enjoy a good time. The response to our marketing produced thirty two runners for this cruise. The cruise we picked sailed on Sunday afternoon at 5:00 P.M.

Most of the runners thought they would have a chance to run on each of the ports of call and of course they could if they wished. However, Mary and I felt they should enjoy the ports of call as well as having a great running experience at some point.

I found a race in Miami for Saturday morning benefiting the Alzheimer's organization. It had five year age groups, nice awards and a great post race party. Every person signed up to run the race! We had thirty two entries.

We flew the group to Ft. Lauderdale on Friday and had to get them from there to our hotel in Miami. It was very cost effective to rent eight cars with four to a car for the drive from Ft. Lauderdale to Miami, then drop the car at the car office in our hotel. People paired off and we rented cars to suit the needs for those four in each group.

Mary and I were paired up with a really nice couple. The men decided the drive was short and we were only driving from the airport to our cruise port hotel so we would rent the smallest, least expensive car available.

I picked up the car and drove back to pick up the other three. What a shock we had when we tried to put four people into the car and their luggage into the trunk. This tiny car would only hold a couple pieces in the trunk. We had about nine or ten pieces with our luggage, running bags and carry-on pieces. We loaded the women in the back seat. They weren't that comfortable just by themselves. I loaded several pieces of luggage on top of them to where we could hardly see either of them. Then I put the fellow in the passenger seat and completely covered him with the rest of the luggage. We couldn't see him either. I could barely see to drive the car because I couldn't see out of the right side or back windows. I did make it safely to our hotel.

We were staying at an elegant Marriott Hotel in the Biscayne Bay area. When I drove in the Bell Captain could hardly contain his laughter. My guess is he probably told everyone he knew about the economy car filled with luggage that revealed three people buried under the luggage.

That night many of us took a cab to the Art Deco area of Miami. Most of us were from West Central Illinois and Eastern Iowa. I don't believe those of us from the cornfields of this area were prepared to see the people of Art Deco.

We saw men and women barely clad with clothes, boa constrictors wrapped around their bodies, hair that was multicolored and piercings in places we could never comprehend.

After the night on the town, we got up early to race! I had rented a motor coach to get us to and from the race. When we arrived, the race director was shocked to see a motor coach full of runners. He clearly did not expect to see a group like ours.

It was a beautiful morning to run. We were not prepared for the higher humidity and heat because this was a January race. Back home we were in the middle of winter and certainly not having this kind of weather.

When the race was over, our group assembled together. The Race Director read the award winner's name, place, time and city. Every time one of our group was announced as a winner we yelled at the top of our lungs! At one point the Race Director stopped and said, "I believe this group from Iowa and Illinois are ringers!"

Out of the thirty two entries we had thirty trophy winners. The only reason the other two did not trophy was because our group had more in the age group than they offered trophies! In other words, they lost to our own people.

I introduced myself to the Race Director. He thanked me for the group and said we had added to the fun and excitement for the day. He also said he had never had anything like it happen at one of his races before.

The cruise turned out to be a great time for everyone. It did not have more organized runs but the group did many memorable things together.

We docked in Ocho Rios, Jamaica and the group climbed the Dunn's River Falls. San Juan, most everyone enjoyed an excursion to El Morrow, the historic old fort. We all gathered to see the beautiful lighting on El Morrow as we sailed away from San Juan at midnight. Cozumel offered a trip to Playa Del Carmen and a Mayan tour of ancient ruins. Finally, in Grand Cayman, we swam with stingrays and everybody went to HELL. Hell is a small community where you can mail postcards home with the postmark, "HELL".

Many of those people continued to travel with us for many years. I don't remember them doing any races when they traveled but I know for certain I always put them into the proper sized rental car!

# No Amount of Planning Replaces Dumb Luck

It's fun to work with your family members. A few years ago our son and daughter-in-law asked us to arrange a custom itinerary for Spain and Italy. They were not interested in a cruise, they wanted a land based with several cities and different transportation options.

We were to fly them to Barcelona for city tours and local sightseeing for several days. From there they wanted to experience the wonders of Italy for a couple weeks. Florence, the Amalfi Coast, Rome, Cinque Terra and finishing in Venice before flying home. This was a very detailed itinerary and we worked on it for over a year, possibly a year and a half.

Many of our friends like to have us travel with them when they travel. It was a spur of the moment decision for us to join two couples on a Mediterranean Cruise. We decided to join with them because we had not experienced all of the Greek Isles we wanted to see and this cruise itinerary included the ones we wanted to visit.

It is always our policy to review documents before we deliver them to clients. When Brian and Kris's documents arrived to our office, Mary and I were enjoying reviewing them and thinking what a good time our kids would have. We looked at each other in surprise because it was clear we would be in Venice at exactly the same time as they were scheduled to be there. It is difficult to explain how hard this would be to arrange on purpose, let alone by accident.

Brian and Kris were arriving in Venice the day before us and staying in a very lovely hotel along one of the canals. We were to arrive the next day to board our cruise ship. Fortunately, we were to board the ship around 2:00 P.M. and the ship was to overnight in Venice and sail late afternoon the day after we boarded. It turned out we had a free evening in Venice!

Before they left on their trip we decided to call each other when we arrived and arrange to have dinner together if possible. After boarding the ship we called and were pleased to find they had located a quaint restaurant close to their hotel for our dinner.

After getting situated on the ship we boarded a water taxi and set out for St. Mark's Square. The taxi docked right close to the Square and the Doge's Palace. We had been given very tentative directions to their hotel that began by walking to the Rialto Bridge, crossing it and then the hotel would be only a couple blocks away.

If you've been to Venice then you know every canal looks the same and every tiny walkway looks the same. We became lost very quickly and had to stop and ask directions to their hotel a couple times. Each stop got us closer and finally we found the hotel with the front door directly three or four feet off a canal.

We entered the hotel and asked for Brian and Kris. Before the desk clerk would even make a call to their room we had to produce our passports. Finally he made a call to their room.

Brian came to greet us and take us to their room. We were quite surprised. Hotels in Venice are small and very very old. Actually they had a suite with a living room, bath and kitchen along with a nice sized bedroom. They were on the ground floor that opened through a sliding door to a private patio.

The patio had a table with four chairs and held a cheese platter and four wine glasses. Kris promptly produced a couple bottles of wine. We had a really nice time with snacks and wine and they were happy to bring us up to date on their trip. They showed us pictures of their trip on their cell phones and we had a nice time prior to leaving for dinner.

Restaurants in Europe do not open for business till early evening and we had the first reservation available which was eight P.M. Of course there was more wine, appetizers, pasta, pizza and salad. Dad was more than happy to pick up the tab for the evening!

We had to be certain our evening finished in time for us to catch the last water taxi back to the ship. European dining is much slower than here in the States. We were worried that finding the way back to the water taxi would be difficult. Leaving the hotel we turned left and in a couple blocks there was the Rialto Bridge. It was a very short walk back to the water taxi stand. We had walked in circles when we tried to locate the hotel earlier. Today it would have been easier with modern GPS Systems.

We caught one of the last water taxis back to the ship. Our ship sailed the next afternoon. Brian and Kris flew back to the States at about the time our ship sailed.

As I said, no amount of planning will replace dumb luck. We did not plan it, it just happened by accident. We will remember it as one of the most memorable evenings we've ever had as we travel the world.

*The Fislar family having dinner in Venice, Italy*

# African Safari in Kenya

We flew from Chicago on August 28th to Nairobi, Kenya by making a stop in London and then on to Nairobi.

We left Chicago on the direct flight to London and arrived about 5:30 A.M. London time after an eight hour flight. Our layover in London was almost the entire day. Again we had a late evening flight to Nairobi. Finally we arrived in Nairobi at 5:30 A.M. Nairobi time after another eight hour exhausting flight.

There were two options for the visa process. We could purchase them before we left, or we could do them right at the airport upon arrival. Using a visa company before we left was very expensive with a great deal of paperwork. The tour company we were using said to simply do it at the airport.

It turned out it was a simple process and not too expensive. The cost was only $50.00 per person for a multiple entry visa which we would need when we returned to Kenya after our tour through Tanzania. Certainly better than the couple hundred dollar cost of the visa company and all the paperwork. Our entire group had visas in just a few minutes.

We were met by our guide as we exited into general population after the visa process and transferred to our hotel, The Nairobi Serena Hotel. We had paid for the previous night so our group would have immediate access to the hotel room and not have to wait till three or four P.M. to check in.

There were seventeen in our group. Most of the group took advantage of the opportunity to get much needed rest after the long exhausting flight. Not so for four of us! Even though we all needed rest, an important mission awaited.

The Rock Island, Illinois Rotary Club has provided water purification units to needy schools in Africa for several years. Clean water in Africa is a major problem. It turned out that several of these units in Nairobi were actually purchased with funds donated by the Rock Island club.

Our group contained three very important members of the Rock Island Rotary. A District Governor, a Past President and a very active committee member.

Weeks before we left, Rotarian Ruth, the District Governor, made contacts through Rotary International and the company that manufactured the water purification units, to actually visit two schools that were using them.

There was a window of only a few hours that this could be accomplished. It happened to be on the day we arrived. Ruth, Marcy and Mary were anxious to do this. I felt I could be helpful not only for their security but also to record the adventure by taking pictures.

It was only an hour or two after we arrived at the hotel that the four of us were picked up by a representative of the manufacturer of the water purification units, and on our way to visit these schools. The trip from a five star hotel to impoverished schools in Nairobi was a shocking eye opener to all of us.

We traveled through areas where the roadsides were blanketed with trash. Women were attempting to wash clothes in streams that were chocolate brown in color. Others were filling water jugs in these same polluted streams to take home for their personal use. Our driver told us the only pure water some children ever get is through the programs provided by Rotary.

The situation was about the same at both schools. The principals of the school showed us the actual units purchased by the Rock Island Rotary and demonstrated how they work. They assembled the students and we listened as they sang and recited poems to us. The students were eager to talk with us and were very happy and loving. I don't believe they had any idea how poor they were. They were just lovely young people making their way in life with what they had. It was a heart warming and memorable experience none of us will ever forget.

*Ruth, Mary & Marcy*

We returned to our five star hotel in time for dinner feeling grateful for this opportunity, but also feeling a little guilty for all we have compared to them.

After dinner our guides had us meet in a lounge to discuss what we could expect the next day. We were told we would see large numbers of animals. The most important information regarded bathroom stops. There are very few places for bathroom stops. Because of the very open and uninhabited areas, we were to expect two to four hours between. In case of unexpected delays it could reach up to five hours!

The next morning we boarded our three 4X4 Land Rovers and left early for our drive across the Great Riff Valley to the Masai Mara Game Reserve. This is where we would experience our first big game drive.

There were thousands and thousands of exotic animals. Herds of zebra, wildebeest, giraffe, elephants, Cape buffalo, gazelles and topi. It is difficult to describe how overwhelmed we were with what we were seeing.

We found an area in the Reserve that did have bathroom facilities and we ate our boxed lunch there. After lunch we did another game drive. Again there were more animals than we expected.

The day ended a few hours before dark when we arrived at the Mara Leisure Lodge located in a beautiful oasis type setting. This will be our home for tonight and tomorrow. We were surprised at the modern facilities. It had a small pool, exercise room and sauna. It also had excellent food. Almost all our meals on the game drives were included.

Everyone turned in early because we were leaving at 4:00 A.M. to the launching site for our hot air balloon ride. This was an optional part of our trip and did cost an additional $550.00 per person! Liftoff was scheduled at the break of dawn.

Having been a pilot for many years myself this really interested me. The winds were gentle at this hour of the morning. That is the big reason we leave so early. This was to be a two to three hour flight and we would enjoy a champagne breakfast after the flight.

It was interesting how they loaded our basket. They laid the basket on its side. There were two compartments in the basket, upper and lower when it was on its side. The top passengers loaded first and the bottom last. About eight on each level. They fired the engine and put hot air into the balloon and let it rise just enough to set it upright. Our entire group was in the same balloon. One couple in our group did not like heights and did not go. They did a short game drive instead.

There were five or six balloons all taking off and in flight together. It turned out to be an amazing experience. We flew over large herds of animals and very interesting terrain. The pilots would raise and lower their balloons as needed to give us a most exciting and interesting experience along with outstanding photo opportunities.

*Our balloon ride*

We had an excellent pilot. When we landed he set the balloon down so gently we could hardly feel it. Some of the others bounced along the ground and had a pretty rough landing. We were very lucky.

Chase vehicles had followed the balloons. Upon landing we boarded our Land Rovers and were taken to an oasis type grove of Acacia trees where they had set up long tables, elegantly set for our champagne breakfast. To be honest that breakfast, out in the wild of the Masai Mara, was one of the better breakfasts we had on the entire trip.

Just FYI, they thought of everything. They had set up portable bathrooms far from the breakfast area for making everyone comfortable after the flight.

We did a short game drive and returned to the Lodge in time for lunch and to pick up the other couple for our afternoon game drive. This game drive we were told would be different from others because we would be seeing mostly giraffes, zebras and lions.

This was an outstanding game drive. Large herds of zebras and giraffes. We did see a number of lions also but in much smaller numbers.

As the afternoon wore on we had journeyed quite a distance from the Lodge and it was getting close to time we must return before darkness would close in on us. Roads in the Masai Mara are at best, only dirt trails without any signage for directions to any destination. We as tourists rely on our guides and their experience. Forget GPS, they don't exist in the Masai Mara.

Usually our three Land Rovers would stay very close to each other. We had just started the return to the Lodge and we were in the rear Land Rover. Our two guides spotted a giraffe that was being stalked by two lions.

We watched this interesting event unfold for several minutes perhaps a half hour. The other two Land Rovers did not see us stay behind and they continued on to the lodge without us.

This was so interesting. The giraffe did escape unharmed. However, we did not see a very violent storm approaching from behind us. All of a sudden it became dark as night. Guides became very concerned and we tried to outrun the storm. The storm overtook us. Thunder, lightning, rain like we had never seen before in our life, and wind so strong we thought the Land

Rover would tip over! Yes, we actually thought we could be tipped over.

Land Rovers are very open so we can see out easily to take pictures. The top hatches can close and the side windows do zip closed. We secured all the openings but the wind and rain was so strong the water poured inside. We were all soaking wet. The guides who speak excellent English very well suddenly began speaking in an African dialect we could not understand.

The dirt roads had washed out to the point they could not be followed. Headlights were not providing near enough light. Our drivers were talking frantically to each other in their language. They tried several routes they thought would get us on a trail to the Lodge.

Repeatedly we were met with dead ends. Either the trail went nowhere or we encountered streams so swollen with water, even our 4X4 Land Rovers could not cross. We were seriously lost in the Masai Mara in this violent storm.

The Land Rover was equipped with a radio and the guides were speaking in their language so we wouldn't know just how serious our position was. We knew that without being told! The radio did no good because there were no markings to tell our location to anyone who would look for us.

The storm had been raging for hours. The drivers said we may have to overnight in the Rover if the rescue teams could not locate us tonight. They told us they would need daytime light to find the way. We were told they had a plan if the storm would let up a little. There were two rescue teams looking for us. If the storm would let up we and the two rescue teams would shine spotlights into the air. They would know their locations and by triangulating they could possibly figure how to locate us.

While the guides were talking on the radio, the rest of us were scanning the skies for lights. It was very difficult to see anything. Finally we spotted a far off light. Our light was finally spotted by them and a few minutes later the other light caught our attention. Our drivers just tried to drive towards the lights and they did the same to our light. One of the rescue teams found a trail to us after many tries and they were able to lead us back to the Lodge.

Upon arrival at the Lodge, we were wet, cold and hungry. It was very late at night. We didn't expect the welcome we received. Our group along with the Lodge Manager and much of his staff lined the entrance to welcome us back. They clapped, yelled and cheered when they saw we were doing okay.

The Lodge Manager said he had held the kitchen staff after their hours in order to feed us when we returned. He did ask me to hurry people along so they could go home after feeding us. That wasn't a problem because we were eager to eat.

A final surprise was waiting for us. After we were almost finished with our main meal the room filled with all of our group and the kitchen staff brought a large cake with WELCOME HOME written on top. There was singing, lots of laughter and a huge sigh of relief.

# African Safari in Tanzania

Today, after an early breakfast we will leave the Mara Leisure Camp and travel to the border town of Isebania to make our way into Tanzania and the Serengeti.

These African countries have some very strange rules. We were able to ride in our Land Rover to the border between Kenya and Tanzania. When we arrived we had to clear the exit visa for Kenya and walk about a hundred yards to the Tanzania entrance where we had to apply for our entry visa.

It was interesting that we had to leave our vehicles in Kenya and pick up new ones in Tanzania. Our drivers transferred our luggage to a new vehicle and were to meet us after we cleared immigration to Tanzania.

More paperwork and this time the visa was $100.00 US. This visa was for unlimited entry for one full year. They would not accept credit cards. It had to be in clean US bills with no writing or rips or tears. Preferably they wanted either fifty or hundred dollar bills. They really didn't want any small bills.

This visa process took much more time than Kenya's. We had to clear three different lines and they were very strict about how you proceeded through each line.

After clearing the immigration we had lunch and drove to the MBUZI MAWE Tent Camp for a two night stay inside the Serengeti National Park.

Everyone knew we were staying a few nights in a Tented Camp. Nobody knew what to expect. Mary was quite anxious about the tent nights. We checked in and were personally escorted to our tent. We could not believe the luxury of these tents. They were very large and had a modern bathroom and showers. There was even a desk in the bedroom area. The bed was a huge king size four poster with some of the finest linens you could imagine.

Our escort had very specific instructions for everyone.

1. You must call the front desk for an escort to move between the lodge and the tents after dark, in either direction.

2. Your tent door must be zipped tightly from the top as far to the bottom as possible. No gaps.
3. You must be very vigilant when walking at any time during the day, especially in early morning hours.

During the night we could hear wildlife moving about around our tent and in the general area of the lodge. No wonder why the need for escorts.

Next morning I woke up early and Mike from our group was just outside his tent which was next door. I was going to walk around a huge boulder about twenty feet from our tents and take some early morning pictures. He yelled at me to stop where I was. He pointed to some tall grass just along side the boulder. Lying down and hidden in the grass with just the top of his head showing was a huge Cape buffalo! Needless to say, I stopped quickly. You must never approach or frighten these wild animals. That would not be good for your health!

The Serengeti did offer more interesting scenery and a wider variety of animals. Leopards, lions, zebras and elephants did not seem to be afraid and they would come very close to our Land Rover. Around every tree or bush was another postcard picture. I took almost 2000 pictures on this trip.

We spent two nights at the Ngorongoro Serena Safari Lodge in the Ngorongoro Crater. This is reputed to be the cradle of civilization where some of man's earliest remains have been found by archaeological expeditions. Moving from the rim to the bottom is over two thousand feet. Lots of bird life and flamingos were found here.

To this point we had seen four of the big five animals in Africa. The elephant, Cape buffalo, lion and leopard were pretty easy to find but we had not seen a rhinoceros to this point. Our search was complete when we found the rhino here in the crater.

Our final stop in Tanzania, on the way back to Kenya was the very famous Arusha Coffee House for lunch. This is a very luxurious Lodge and Coffee House. We found out that several American Presidents have stayed here. They have good taste because not only was the Lodge beautiful, but also the luncheon was excellent.

Returning into Kenya was much easier because we already had the visas. However we had to unload the

Land Rovers and transfer all our belongings to the Kenya vehicles.

The return to Nairobi took us through Amboseli National Park. We were hoping for a clear view of Mt. Kilimanjaro. It was clear at the base but the summit was shrouded by clouds which the drivers told us was very common. Amboseli National Park was very interesting with many very different animals.

We did overnight at the famous Satao Elerai Lodge which directly overlooks the Amboseli Plain and Mount Kilimanjaro before our return day to Nairobi.

Our last couple days and nights would be very filled with activities. The night we returned from Amboseli we checked into the Nairobi Serena Hotel again.

We had time to refresh ourselves and have dinner at the world renowned Carnivori Restaurant. They are known the world over for their "Beast of a Feast" and the drink created in their restaurant that is the national drink of Kenya, called "Dawa." This drink consists of lime, sugar, vodka and honey.

The Beast of a Feast includes meat from some of the most exotic animals in the world. Crocodile, ostrich and zebra just to name a few. They also have the Nyama Choma which is their name for BBQ meats.

Waiters are dressed in colorful outfits, have big smiles and are very attentive. They circulate throughout the restaurant with large skewers of exotic meats and slice off whatever you want. This was the most exotic dining experience we have ever seen or heard about. Bartenders come to the table and have all ingredients for the Dawa on a tray strapped to their waist. You never have to wait to order a Dawa and you get to watch them make it at your table.

Our final day in Nairobi was also a highlight of the trip. We had arranged a day at the David Sheldrick Wildlife Trust. This is an orphanage for elephants that are rescued from the wild. After they have been rehabilitated they are released back into the wild. We were able to see them up close and personal.

Next we went to the Giraffe Center. They essentially do the same thing as the elephant trust but we had a lot more interaction with the giraffes. We could feed them and if you were brave enough, and I was, you could put a carrot stick in your teeth and they would take it from you with a flick of their tongue. Giraffes are gentle animals and not afraid of people, especially at this Center.

I cannot close a chapter about Kenya and Tanzania without a short discussion about their roads. There are very few paved highways in either country. If you can imagine the very worst road you've been on in our country you're not even close to how rough roads are in these countries. Besides that the drivers race over these roads at barbaric speeds.

Once you leave the villages or cities you travel these dirt paths with large ruts and holes at the high speeds. It is certainly the most bone jarring ride you will ever experience. It's this simple. If you wish to see the wonders of Kenya and Tanzania be prepared for this rough ride!

# Victoria Falls, Zimbabwe

Some of our group flew home directly after the afternoon at the Giraffe Center leaving on evening flights. The rest of us returned to our hotel for a night's rest before an early morning flight from Nairobi, Kenya to the country of Zambia. We had to purchase visas and clear immigration in Zambia. It was only a ten minute drive to the Zimbabwe border where we had to purchase visas and clear immigration again. It wasn't difficult but it was time consuming with long lines at each border. Visas cost $50.00 per person at each border.

Victoria Falls is one of the seven natural wonders of the world. We were anxious to check into the Victoria Falls Safari Lodge, freshen up and take an amazing sunset dinner cruise with up close views of the Falls. Our Captain also took us close to the shore line to see wildlife native only to this area.

Next morning we took a guided walking tour of the falls. We happened to be there at their driest season, however, the falls were a most impressive sight. As we were at the last overlook and almost ready to go back to the Lodge, everyone was looking straight out at the falls and I happened to look off to one side through some trees and we ended our tour of the falls with a view of the most beautiful rainbow that was created by the falls that you've ever seen! It is a lasting memory of Victoria Falls.

We returned to our Lodge just in time to sit on our balcony and watch as the park rangers were ready to feed the vultures. They do this every afternoon at the same time and the vultures know this. They come to roost waiting for the feeding to begin. When the Rangers begin the feeding they do it quickly and get out of the way very quickly. It is a vicious food fight among the vultures until every scrap of meat is gone.

That evening we had reservations at the Boma Dinner and Drum Show. It consisted of authentic African entertainment and food. The moment you arrive the fun begins. You are ceremoniously dressed in your chitenge (sarong). Immediately after you're dressed, you will be welcomed by traditional African dancers and your face will be painted. Men receive stripes giving them the look of traditional African warriors. Women are painted with dots on their cheeks signifying the beauty of African women.

The evening consisted of a four course dinner beginning with our waiter bringing to the table a platter of IVULAMPHIMBO, known in English as starters. The smoked crocodile tail was good, followed with peppered impala and apricot fruit on a skewer.

Tonight's second course, IMBHIDA YABELUMGU, from the buffet was salads, dressings and breads. Make your own salad with all the usual salad fixings. Fruits and vegetables are big in African diets. The salad bar also included UMHLUZI WALAMHLA which we called the soup of the day.

Course number three was EMAWOSWENI WEBOMA, the main course. This included a wide selection of grilled game meats including warthog 'pumba' steak, beef, pork, fish and marinated chicken. The buffet included so many vegetable side dishes it's impossible to describe. Also included was a complete vegetarian menu.

Finally, we enjoyed KWEZINAMBITHAYO. You know this as dessert. The selection was varied and delicious. I'm a dessert person and I couldn't begin to sample them all.

There were numerous activities going on during dinner and prior to the main show. Mbira music, traditional dancers, story tellers and souvenir sellers to name a few.

All of the food listed here came from their souvenir menu we brought home with us.

Highlighting the evening was their world renowned, energetic and interactive entertainment that began promptly at 8:45 P.M. We were told this is the only show of its kind in Zimbabwe. We were all given a djembe drum and we were taught a few rhythms so we could participate in the show.

To finish the evening's entertainment, music was provided for those who wished to dance. Finally, we all had the opportunity to get a certificate telling the world we were brave enough to eat a special worm. I forget the worm's name but it is significant to note, even the vegetarian in our group has a certificate!

Next afternoon we cleared immigration again at the Zimbabwe and Zambia borders in order to return to the airport for our return flight back home.

Our journey was from Zambia to Nairobi, Kenya to Paris, France and then a direct flight to Chicago. Almost thirty-six hours of flights. Our limo picked our group up at O'Hare in Chicago for another three hour ride home.

Victoria Falls was a perfect way to end a most exciting and exotic journey. If you are at Victoria Falls, you absolutely do not want to miss The Boma Dinner and Drum Show.

# Ireland – St. Patrick's Day

The Quad Cities has one of the most talented and diversified musical groups I've ever seen. My mom sang with Red Foley in the early forties and I've been around theater my entire life. The Quad Cities Bucktown Revue is based on the format of old time radio variety shows. Every show is different and when you attend it's what, I believe Forest Gump said, "it's like a box of chocolates, you never know what you're going to get." The talent is amazing.

Mary and I have been a sponsor of the group for many years and we asked the owner if we could promote a group to Ireland for a week over St. Patrick's Day. We developed an itinerary, working with Wendy Hager at CIE Tours. She is simply the best there is for designing a custom Ireland Group Tour. We presented it and it was approved.

We did not expect the response we got. Many of the cast of Bucktown Revue signed on right away and said they were taking their instruments. We filled two full motor coaches!

The group flew from Chicago direct to Dublin. The only issue we had was we had so many instruments and the flight attendants didn't seem to know how to handle them. We left on March 15th and arrived in Dublin early morning on the 16th.

Upon arrival we were taken to the Coachman's Inn for a traditional Irish breakfast. We met our local guide there and after breakfast did a city tour that included the Book of Kells and of course after a Guinness tour a trip to the roof top bar for samples of Guinness!

After we checked in for our two night stay at the Camden Court Hotel, dinner was provided and was over early. We asked the hotel manager if our friends from Bucktown could get out their instruments and set up in the hotel lobby.

They were okay with it even though their bar had music that night. The Bucktown people had standing room only in the lobby. The hotel was happy because the crowd purchased a lot of drinks. In fact they finally had servers work the lobby and they did far more business than the lounge group was doing. They played for hours and the crowd clapped and cheered each song!

The next day was St. Patrick's Day. Mary and I did it right! We purchased grandstand tickets for the entire group. If you're going to go to Dublin for St. Patrick's Day, buy the grandstand tickets. Our buses took the group to only a block from the grandstand viewing area. We had an entire section to ourselves with comfortable chairs and a canopy overhead. It certainly beat standing for hours in the sun or possibly rain, with crowds of people pushing and shoving for position. Our seats for the parade were absolutely worth the price.

We planned no other activities for the day. After dinner the Bucktown Revue group played their instruments again in the lobby. The crowd that night was larger than the previous night and the hotel did a land office business from the bar. The Bucktown Revue was a very big hit in Dublin on St. Patrick's Day.

We did a visit the next day to Blarney Castle. Most of our people kissed the Blarney Stone to acquire the gift of, "eloquence." I thought our group already had it but it couldn't hurt to get more. The rest of the day was spent touring the scenery and country side of the area around the Rock of Cashel. We stayed that night at the Imperial Hotel in Cork. A band the hotel had hired did not show up to play that night. Our group played for a couple hours. Again they were a big hit although the crowds were much smaller than in Dublin. The hotel manager said he couldn't believe how lucky he was to have our group there and be able to play for him. I thought he should have paid them. He didn't but it was okay. The Bucktown Revue had enjoyed themselves.

Thursday we toured the one hundred miles of the Ring of Kerry where we had numerous photo stops. We found our way to The Killarney Towers Hotel in Killarney. My friend Mike had made only one request before we left. He said the group wanted to play in a real Irish Pub. I had worked with Wendy at CIE and she had found a Pub in Killarny for the group to play. It was called the Leprechaun Pub. It was a small Pub but the group got to play for a couple hours. Needless to say, Bucktown brought the house down! The Leprechauns kept asking for more. Bucktown had a wonderful time, but the bar had a great night too because our group enjoyed a lot of their Irish cheer!

We toured the Cliffs of Moher on Friday. Its seven hundred foot tall cliffs were bathed in sunlight and a marvelous sight to see. After a couple hours we left the Cliffs for our scenic trip to Bunratty. Our last night was arranged to be a very memorable one for everyone as well as a lot of fun. The Bucktown Revue folks will not play their instruments tonight. It's their turn to be entertained.

Everyone had wanted a chance to stay in a castle. Tonight we are at the Bunratty Castle Hotel. I'd suggest everyone touring Ireland should make it a priority to stay at this hotel, it's just that much fun.

The most well known and entertaining evening is the medieval style banquet in Bunratty Castle. This banquet is an interactive banquet with a great deal of audience participation. A King and Queen are selected from the audience to reign over the evening's proceedings.

Mary and I were the only two at the banquet who knew in advance the King and Queen selection had been rigged. We had worked with Wendy at CIE Tours to arrange with the Bunratty management to select Mike and Carol of Bucktown Revue, as the King and Queen.

Mike and Carol reigned over the evening in royal fashion. It was a hilariously entertaining evening. Bunratty was the perfect way to end our trip to Ireland. Our friends at Bucktown and clients relive this adventure every St. Patrick's Day. The next morning we traveled to Dublin for our return flight to Chicago, but the memories live on.

# Grand Canyon

Do you know what you want for dinner two years from today? Or breakfast the next morning? That's the choice you need to make if you make reservations to hike to the bottom of the Grand Canyon and stay overnight at the Phantom Ranch.

The National Park system requires everyone to register if they are going to hike the Canyon. When we made reservations to stay at the Phantom Ranch we had to make reservations two years to the day in advance. They now have some kind of lottery and the time is only fifteen months in advance. Mostly now it is done online.

Making reservations was very difficult because they were getting thousands of calls every day. The reservation system opened at 7:00 A.M. central time. I began calling at five minutes before and had the phone on redial. With each busy signal I immediately hung up and hit redial.

I was actually shocked to hear the phone ring and be answered. We were calling on August 2nd, which is the day before our anniversary because we wanted to hike down and overnight on the second of August and hike out of the Canyon on August 3rd, our anniversary.

We had choices of sleeping arrangements at Phantom Ranch. They have a men's dorm and a women's dorm. They also have a few free-standing cabins. We opted for the cabin. You have to order your meals at the time you make the reservation at Phantom Ranch. You have to pay in full at the time of the reservation for meals and the cabin. There was no refund if you found you could not hike the Canyon on the date you had reserved.

The meal choices were either steak or a miner's stew for dinner. We ordered the miner's stew and the breakfast was the standard sausage or bacon and egg so we ordered and paid the bill for the meals and the cabin.

Two years passed quickly. We flew to Phoenix on August 1st, rented a car and drove to the Grand Canyon. I had made reservations for August 1st at the Maswick Lodge in the Park. It was a small cabin and very rustic but we had to be there on the 1st to check in with the Park Rangers for orientation.

We asked a lot of questions and the Rangers were very helpful. They told us it would be best if we went down on the South Kaibab Trail and returned to the top on the Bright Angel Trail. We asked if we would need hiking poles but the Rangers said they would not be necessary. They told us it would take about eight hours to get to the bottom and would take about twelve hours to return to the top. They said an early start was necessary because August is the hottest time of the year at the Grand Canyon.

Hydration is a huge issue. There is no water available on the South Kaibab Trail. Temperatures were forecast to be between 100 and 110 degrees. They were right on, as it was 105 degrees each day we were on the trail. Being under hydrated could cause serious health issues or even death. There is no shade at all on the South Kaibab Trail.

This was the only time I've seen Mary use a backpack but it was very necessary. She carried a change of clothes for each of us and some snack items in hers. I packed thirty twenty-ounce bottles of Gatorade in my backpack. It was quite heavy to start but we would be sweating profusely and we had to replace fluids often. It got lighter as we went down the trail.

Rules are very strict. Anything you carry down you must carry out. You can be fined for dropping litter on the trails. Mule trains have the right of way. If you encounter a mule train you must move off the trail and let them pass. You must not bother the wildlife or the foliage.

The Rangers told us we had to park in a special lot and take a complimentary shuttle bus to the trail head of the South Kaibab Trail. We had to catch the bus at 4:00 A.M. At the trail we had to sign in with our departure time and when we expected to return out of the Canyon.

From the rim to the floor of the Grand Canyon is almost five thousand feet straight down. South Kaibab Trail is over seven miles of dangerous switch backs from trail head to the Phantom Ranch.

It was just before 5:00 A.M. when we entered the trail head of the South Kaibab Trail. It was still quite dark and we had to move carefully on the trail. The trail itself was very narrow, usually only room for one person and it was very rocky and had lots of very loose gravel and shale. We had to be very careful because there were no railings and the drop on each side would be fatal because you would fall several hundred feet if you went over the edge.

A turned ankle or a fall of any kind would be a disaster. The Rangers told us rescue by helicopter is about the only way to get an injured person out. They also told us the cost for the helicopter is usually about ten thousand dollars!

As the sun came up and it began to get brighter we could see glorious colors on the walls of the Canyon. The colors changed as we progressed downward and the sun rose higher. Unless you hike the Canyon you will never see the beauty we experienced that day.

The trail was indeed treacherous and it became worse when a drizzling rain made the rocks on the trail very slippery. The rain made every step a potential accident. The rain lasted about an hour. Heat and humidity were also an issue, especially since the rain.

We progressed downward until we came to a large overlook. We could see the Colorado River as it flows through the Canyon. From here we could see our trail moved through a tunnel and exited onto a bridge only wide enough for a person, perhaps a mule. After crossing the bridge it was only a short distance to the river and the bottom of the Grand Canyon.

A sign said it was only a half mile to the Phantom Ranch. The path was narrow with a great deal of weeds and brush growing on each side. We were thrilled to be so close to our destination when all of a sudden three unhappy wild turkeys came out of the brush and blocked our way.

The turkeys were not thrilled to see us. It goes without saying we weren't thrilled to see them either. We were tired and just wanted to get to the Phantom Ranch. I told Mary we just needed to take baby steps forward. No sudden moves, just creeping forward taking stops every few feet. I figured they would eventually leave the trail. Turkeys must speak English because they were doing the same thing we were. It was a stalemate, they must have had a nest nearby and were protecting it. We were patient and finally were able to move past them. They followed us almost to the Phantom Ranch before they gave up on us.

It took us far less time to go down than the Rangers said it would. We did it in five and a half hours. We really could have used the hiking poles. They had a small shop where you could purchase a few items. We purchased poles for the return trip. It would have been nice to have them on the way down.

Facilities at the Ranch were a little primitive but our cabin was comfortable and clean. It had running water and a bathroom but no shower. It was a short walk to the bath house that had different facilities for men and women.

At dinner, which was excellent, we discussed our return hike the next day with others that had hiked the Bright Angel Trail before. Most said it would take us the twelve hours the Rangers had told us. The trail itself is just a tenth of a mile less than ten miles. It has slight elevations for the first five miles but the last half of the trail has an almost three thousand foot increase in elevation. The Canyon rim is about 6300 feet so we would be climbing the hardest part in the heat of the day at an elevation a little over a mile high.

We were scheduled to leave Phantom Ranch just after breakfast, maybe 7:00 A.M. Our anniversary dinner reservation was at 4:00 P.M. at the El Tovar Lodge where we also had a room reservation for that night. Leaving after breakfast would cause us to miss our dinner reservation. The Ranch was very willing to pack a box lunch for each of us and give us some fruit when we told them we would be moving our start time to 5:00 A.M.

The trip between Phantom Ranch and the Indian Gardens rest area is just half way and that went pretty well. Indian Gardens had water and restrooms. It also had benches to sit on to rest. Indian Gardens is a favorite for people that want to hike a part of the Canyon but either cannot get reservations or do not have the strength to go completely down and back.

Mary and I were getting quite tired by this time and we decided not to sit down. We were afraid we wouldn't be able to move again. We really needed to be back for our dinner reservation.

Those last four miles up hill in the heat and altitude were very difficult. Rest stops along the trail were necessary. About a mile past Indian Gardens we saw a helicopter land on a very small rocky area. A woman had fallen off a donkey and fractured her hip and was being taken out by helicopter. We had to wait while a two-wheeled stretcher took her to the helicopter for her ride to a hospital.

Mary and I were both exhausted when we reached the rim. We drank the last of our Gatorade at the top. We drank fifteen twenty-ounce bottles each way and we needed every ounce to stay properly hydrated. We were also pleased with ourselves because we made the return trip under nine hours!

Just as we reached the rim the bus that would take us back to where our car was parked drove off without us. They run on the half hour and we could not wait for the next one. It was a mile from where we were to our car. Yes, we walked to the car!

We arrived at the El Tovar Lodge just before 3 P.M. The anniversary reservation was at 4 P.M. I went to the restaurant and told the lady handling reservations that we had just gotten out of the Canyon, we needed time to shower and rest a little and could she move us to 7 P.M.? No, it is fully booked. I shook her hand with a ten-dollar bill in it and said I could wait a few minutes if she would see if she could find room for us at 7 P.M.

I don't know how she did it, but she motioned me to her and said we have a 7 P.M. reservation. Again, I thanked her and asked if maybe a window table with a view of the Canyon would be available. "Oh no not possible." I shook her hand with another ten-dollar bill and she said she'd see what she could do.

We could barely walk. I had run marathons that did not hurt me as much as that hike down and back in the Grand Canyon. After our shower and a little rest, we appeared at 7:00 P.M. for dinner. The lady whispered to me that she hoped we would enjoy our window table. I shook her hand again with another ten-dollar bill and asked her if the Chef could fix a special dessert for us.

Our anniversary concluded that evening with the waiters singing to us as they presented us with a cookie that was about sixteen inches in diameter decorated with, "Happy Anniversary, Dick & Mary".

Anniversaries are very special to us. This is just one of our many wonderful memories, but it is a very special memory.

# Budapest to Amsterdam

We believe the most interesting river cruise in Europe begins in Budapest and ends in Amsterdam. This is a fifteen day cruise on three rivers, the Danube, Main and Rhine. The most important cities in Europe have been built on rivers and this cruise gives you insight into many of those cities.

You can go either direction. Either Amsterdam to Budapest or Budapest to Amsterdam. There is good reason to prefer the itinerary cruising from Budapest to Amsterdam. We suggest flying to Budapest at least a day prior to the cruise. Being a day early gives you a chance to rest and be ready for the long trip ahead of you. It also will give you some additional time to spend time on your own exploring the sights and restaurants that are not offered by the cruise line.

The biggest benefit comes at the end of the cruise. The flight home from Amsterdam is much shorter and has far better flight schedules than ones from Budapest.

We arrived in Budapest too late for the cruise ship's transfer because we had encountered some flight delays. We didn't have their currency but the man at the taxi stand told us not to worry; the taxi would take a credit card. Okay, we get in the taxi and after a few minutes he pulls into a bank parking lot and directs me to an ATM. He didn't take a card but he knew where the ATM was located. We got some local currency, paid the taxi and checked in on the ship. This was not our first trip to Budapest so we did not fly in the recommended day early.

Next morning the cruise line provided a city tour. After we returned to the ship from the tour we decided to change clothes and go for a run. Being typical tourists we ran along the Danube River and we were a couple miles away from the ship. I was watching the Parliament building, not watching where I was going, and stepped into a large pot hole in the sidewalk. My ankle swelled to twice its size and of course it was a very long way back to the ship.

I always carry a camera when we run and when we finally arrived back to the ship I told Mary to stand under the ship's name on the gangway for a picture. A crewman rushed out, put his arm around Mary's shoulder and said,

"Can I be in the picture?" I said, "sure" figuring I'd delete him later. It turned out he was the Captain! It's a good picture and I didn't delete him.

We sailed that evening after dark and passed by the parliament building that was beautifully bathed in lights. The Parliament in Budapest is one of the most photographed buildings in Europe.

*Parliament Building in Budapest*

Along the Danube you will not only find the major cities of Europe, you will also find quaint little villages. Durnstein is one of those quaint villages. It is one of the highest visited tourist destinations on the Danube. The reason for that is the beautiful church on the riverbank and the photogenic surroundings.

Many of the passengers were thrilled to go through the locks. Being from the Quad Cities and only a mile from the locks on the Mississippi we enjoyed them, but after sixty eight sets of locks between Budapest and Amsterdam I believe everyone did lose some enthusiasm.

Melk is a monastery built high on a cliff. Again, this is a highly photographed site. They were extremely proud of their Linden tree grove. Mary and I have a Linden tree in our lawn that was at least four or five times taller than any of theirs but we didn't have the heart to say it to them. The monastery when viewed from below is quite impressive and also an excellent photo op.

***Monastery in Melk***

One unforgettable evening was an optional evening Mozart Concert in Vienna. Uniworld had excellent seats reserved for us. We were greeted at the door of a beautiful concert hall with trays of champagne. The string ensemble was excellent and they were joined by a couple that waltzed in synchronization to the classical music. Anyone that missed this evening would have missed one of the most wonderful evenings of entertainment on the entire cruise. If you go to Vienna please don't miss this. You will thank me.

On a previous trip we had stopped in Passau and were very happy to return. We did a walking tour that finished with free time in the city square. This was perfect for us. Last time here in Passau we had found a pastry shop that had some of the finest pastry you can imagine. It took us a while but we found it again. We enjoyed several pastries with coffee and we took a bag of goodies back to the ship with us!

One thing we like about Europe is that every city has marvelous bakeries with large displays of pastry offerings in very large windows. It is seldom you will find this in the United States.

Passau is a historic city and the walk uphill to its fortress is worth the walk. We love good views and the view from above is marvelous.

Every city on this trip is filled with history, beautiful churches and exciting tourist destinations. Honestly we toured so many churches and cathedrals on this trip it became hard to keep them straight. These historic buildings are hundreds and thousands of years old. It is so satisfying to walk in the footsteps of the famous people and enjoy these historic buildings.

The United States does not preserve their heritage in the same way as Europe. We have a history of demolishing older historical buildings instead of refurbishing them. We have a wonderful history, but the buildings we have to show our past heritage are disappearing rapidly.

The Main River was interesting because of a manmade canal that connects the Danube, Main and Rhine Rivers. Our Captain said we should be outside on deck to see the canal built over a huge valley carrying the entire river's content. It was an engineering feat like we'd never seen before.

When you are on the Rhine river between Rudesheim and St. Gorhausen you will see castles built high on the hills. They are about a half mile apart but on alternating sides of the river. This goes on for many miles. Vineyards from the top of the hills run completely down to the river's edge along this entire section of the river. I guarantee you will not forget this part of Europe.

Rudesheim is a very famous city known for the handmade cuckoo clocks and a recently constructed cable car ride to the top of the mountain close by. We have some friends that have purchased clocks while on stops here from cruise ships. We have ridden the cable car and it is a very fun and interesting ride.

Cruising the rivers of Europe is comfortable on the luxurious ships. Food is excellent, nightly entertainment is good and the crew on these ships make you feel very special. Cruise directors usually give a nightly talk before dinner giving information about the next day's port and activities.

You will never forget the vacation you take on a river cruise!

# Running on New Year's Eve

I've mentioned elsewhere in this book how we feel about New Year's Eve and how we prefer things other than house parties. For at least ten years we would fly someplace in the United States and run a race. Most of them were at the stroke of midnight on New Year's Eve... Sometimes it would be an early morning run New Year's Day.

When I look back at the cost of airline tickets, hotels, car rentals and entry fees it probably was by most standards a very expensive way to dodge house parties. It was however, a great deal of fun and we had some memorable experiences on New Year's.

DALLAS, TEXAS. This race was to start at 8:00 A.M. on New Year's Day in White Rock Park. We got up about 5:30 A.M. and I went onto our balcony to check the weather. It was beautiful, about sixty-five degrees, which is perfect to race. We dressed in shorts and T-shirts so we would not be too warm running.

We arrived at the race site around 7:00 A.M. and it seemed to be much cooler. By the 8:00 A.M. start, the temps had dropped to about forty degrees. This is still okay to run in the clothes we were wearing. It was a five mile run. The gun had barely started the race when it began a cold rain! The further we ran, the colder the rain. Half way through the race it began a freezing rain and sleet!

When we crossed the finish line we ran to our parked car, soaking wet and freezing. We turned on the heater full blast. We were absolutely frozen and we stayed inside the car until the awards ceremony. Mary and I both won our age divisions! We collected our trophies and rushed to our hotel to change clothes and pack our belongings. Our flight was to be a late afternoon flight.

After turning in our rental car we rushed to the customer service desk and asked to board an earlier flight. This flight left Dallas around one P.M. Our flight attendant announced they closed the airport just after we took off. It turned out to be one of the worst ice storms Dallas had seen in years.

COLUMBUS, OHIO. This race was set to start on the stroke of midnight. It was a 5K run through the city streets beginning and ending on a high school track. We remember this race because as we arrived we could see the bright lights of the football field. It had just begun a light snowfall and with the snow falling through the lights it was one of the most beautiful scenes for the start and end of a race.

They had a very nice post race party. We stayed around for some very good food, talked with the locals and enjoyed a glass of champagne before retiring to our hotel.

Once again, Mary and I had won our age divisions. One local could not believe we had flown to Columbus just to race at midnight. He had finished in second place behind me and I was told he was a little upset because, "Those out of town people took our trophies!"

JACKSONVILLE, FLORIDA. This was a very big race but it was run early evening, at 5:00 P.M., on New Year's Eve. Mary was second and I was third in our age divisions but we were happy because of the large number of entrants. The more entries, the more difficult it is to trophy.

By entering the race we were given the opportunity to purchase very good tickets to the Cotton Bowl game New Year's Day. We enjoyed the game and spent the next day touring St. Augustine in Northeast Florida.

ST. LOUIS, MISSOURI. We were supposed to race in St. Louis at midnight. The next day we were to take an early flight to Cancun, Mexico. The forecast was to be far below zero with snow at race time. Those wimps canceled the race.

Our hotel was close to the airport but in a good area to run. Just prior to midnight, Mary and I dressed for a run and went downstairs. The doorman looked at us as if we were crazy! He asked us if we knew it was four below zero and snowing.

Of course we did, but we were determined to run at midnight. As we ran through the neighborhoods, fireworks lit up the sky. The fireworks and the snow was a beautiful setting for entering a New Year.

Upon return to the hotel the doorman rushed to open the door for us and told us how glad he was to see us return. He truly couldn't believe we could run in this kind of weather. We had some champagne in the room and enjoyed the New Year's beginning. Our flight was a six A.M. flight. We had to be at the airport at four A.M. so we didn't get a lot of sleep.

I must admit we enjoyed the four days we spent in Cancun beginning the next day a little more.

SAN FRANCISCO, CALIFORNIA. From everything we could learn, the race at midnight in San Francisco had the very best post race New Year's party in the United States. The food was to be outstanding combined with champagne, bands and a huge awards ceremony.

We flew out a couple days before New Year's and did some major sightseeing. One thing we did that was super cool was, we ran both directions across the Golden Gate Bridge! That is an experience every runner should have. We rode the street cars, ate great food at the Fisherman's Wharf and rested up for the big event.

Our race was to begin at 11:50 P.M. for a 5K race (3.1 miles) and we would run into the new year. Fireworks would go off as we ran and of course we looked forward to the post race party and awards ceremony.

We drove to the area under the Golden Gate called the Presidio where the race was to start. We arrived about 9:00 P.M. for the 11:50 P.M. race. We were told if we did not arrive early we would not find a parking spot. We arrived quite early and found a great parking spot very close to the starting line.

We had not been parked more than a half hour when it began to rain. It was what my grandpa called, "a frog strangler." The rain was coming in sheets and the wind was blowing so hard the rain appeared to be sideways. We stayed in the car hoping to see it let up.

Not so, it continued to rain right up to race time. Mary and I did not bring rain gear for running. People were lining up at the starting line. We joined them and the race went off on time. At midnight the fireworks went off overhead. How they did that in the driving rain I'll never know! We finished the race together and were lucky our car was so close to the finish line. We've never been that wet in our life!

San Francisco was supposed to be the finest post race New Year's party ever. It was completely canceled. No food, no band, and no awards because the timing equipment failed during of the storm.

Needless to say, the race wasn't what we had expected. It's a funny story to tell and when we look back it was a good time. Plus, we did miss a house party.

NEW YORK CITY. When you say New Year's and New York in the same sentence, the first thing most people think of is Times Square. We took a group of runners to New York City for a race at the stroke of midnight in a most unlikely place.

Most people would not consider running in Central Park at midnight. We wouldn't either usually, but we joined several thousand hearty souls for a five mile race at midnight. It was snowing lightly and the temperature was only in the twenties.

The starting line was just outside one of the most elegant and expensive restaurants in New York. The Tavern On The Green. Limos were dropping off women in elegant gowns and men in tuxedos. A large window of the restaurant faces out into Central Park and it was beautiful to look inside and see how the very rich and famous were spending their New Year's Eve. Even though we were enjoying watching them, I don't know how they felt to see several thousand runners in their tights and sweatshirts just outside their window.

Mary and I had decided we would run with each other so we would not be separated. That was a good idea because it was very dark and so many people. I don't know how we would have found each other if we had not stayed together.

The race began at exactly midnight and we ran the paths in the park. There was a nice display of fireworks. Every race has water stops on the course to hydrate runners as they race. The water stops in Central Park that night had two choices. You could have water, but the tables with the champagne were getting the most action!

This group stayed a couple extra days in New York to do some tours. We took the ferry to the Statue of Liberty and Ellis Island, we took a Gray Line tour of the city, and we took in a couple Broadway shows.

I began running when I was only about twelve so I've done it most of my life. Mary and I have been running together for over thirty years. It is always great when couples can enjoy things together. What has really been fun is sharing our passion with our running friends when they can travel with us.

# Spain & Portugal

Spain and Portugal has always been an area of Europe that I feel has been overlooked. There are many wonderful places to visit in both countries. Mary really liked the idea and she researched several companies. Her favorite itinerary was with Insight Vacations. Our Sales Manager Cynthia O'Kelly was the top sales person worldwide for the entire company.

Cynthia put together a PowerPoint presentation that was personalized just for us. It was very very good and our clients that we had invited left the evening energized and ready to travel to Spain and Portugal. A group quickly formed!

We flew American Airlines on September 1 at 11:05 A.M., Moline to Chicago and had a direct flight Chicago to Madrid at 4:40 P.M. arriving 7:45 A.M. the next morning. Immediately after we cleared immigration and customs we were met by the Insight transfer company.

One lady needed wheelchair assistance because of the long walk to our motor coaches. The airport provided a Red Cap to push her and the husband went along with her. Wheelchairs had to take a different route. We gave instructions where they were to meet the rest of the group so we could board the coaches to the hotel. For some reason they never appeared at the meeting point!

The Red Cap's English, or my Spanish must not have been clear. The group found places to sit and wait. I went on a search of the airport to find them. One thing that is never possible is to re-enter the immigration area after you've left it. Being the silver tongued person that I am, I pleaded with the guards to re-enter to search. Finally I found a sympathetic supervisor. He made a public address both in English and in Spanish. Of course nobody responded. He allowed me to re-enter and I finally found the couple and was able to escort them to where the rest of the group was waiting.

This entire process took about an hour and a half. Mary was concerned that I was also lost. They had left their Insight Documents with their luggage and the luggage was with us. Without being found they would not have known the hotel or had a way to get there. Of course, we would never leave without everybody. It was a stressful time however and we were very relieved when we found them and were able to move on to the Miguel Angel Hotel.

Our rooms were not available until 3:00 P.M. and we had arrived just before lunch. The group had lunch and settled into the bar to relax until check-in. Some people relaxed quite a bit more in the bar than others!

At check-in we were assigned our rooms and given the information as to where and when for our welcome dinner and to meet our tour guide, Mr. Bradley Dick.

The next morning we leave early for visits to Toledo and Granada. Our first stop is Toledo. One thing I remember most is the view of the city from a few miles away. We stopped high on a bluff that looked down on the city for a photo stop. Looking down on the city is impressive because the city sits high on a bluff overlooking the Rio Tagus. The skyline is dotted with steeples of Catedral de Toledo, one of the top ten Cathedrals in Spain and the Alcazar Museum that is built on the highest point of the city. Alcazar was originally built as a fortress in

1085 and was used as a Roman Palace around 300 AD. This photo op certainly gave our people some postcard photos. Our guide said, "Now that you've seen all the Churches and Cathedrals from this angle, you can honestly say, HOLY TOLEDO!"

In the middle ages Toledo had large populations of Muslims, Jews and Christians and they were able to exist without conflict and in fact worked together sharing their information. In 1968 Toledo was named a UNESCO site, siting the cooperation between cultural differences and religions.

The Catedral de Toledo is a great example of Gothic Architecture and was large and beautiful inside. We moved on to the Alcazar. Originally built as a fortress, used as a Roman Palace it is now an army museum. Uniforms and weaponry throughout the history of Spain is the main focus and was very interesting. Our final stop in Toledo was the Church of Santo Tome where we enjoyed a display of El Greco's famous works of art.

Late afternoon, we moved on to Granada and checked into our Hotel Vincci Albayzin. The group had dinner together at the hotel.

Mary and I had been to Granada before to visit the Alhambra. It is only an hour from the Mediterranean Coast. We had visited as part of a shore excursion provided by a cruise ship. The Alhambra is one of the most visited sites in Spain.

The Alhambra has had many uses over its long history. The Romans had a history here before it was constructed as a fortress in 889 AD. It became a Royal Palace in 1333 AD. Brad told us Christopher Columbus received his commission for exploration from Spain here in 1492. It is well known for its Islamic architecture. It is also a UNESCO World Heritage Site.

We move through the very scenic drive on our way to Seville this afternoon where the group does a walking tour through the Santa Cruz Quarter enjoying the small squares and parks.

Two UNESCO-designated sites were part of our tour in Seville. The Alcazar Palace and Gardens and the La Giralda Cathedral which was a Mosque that later became a Cathedral. It is the final resting place of Christopher Columbus.

After the visit to the Cathedral, Brad, our guide, had arranged to have a group picture taken. The temperature this day set a new high record in Seville. It was said to be 113 or 114 degrees Fahrenheit and everyone agreed they had never been so hot in their lives. A great part of today's tours was walking and it was very uncomfortable.

*It was 113 or 114°F when we took this picture.*

Seville has always been important because it is the only river seaport in Spain. Ferdinand Magellan departed from here for his successful circumnavigation of the earth.

Our evening ended with the group having dinner and enjoyed an energetic Flamenco show at our Hotel Ayre. Thankfully it was air conditioned!

Everyone had a free day in Seville the next day. Many of us met for dinner outdoors in the evening. It was nice to have down time after the heat yesterday.

Spain is famous for their Spanish Hams. We travel today from Seville to Lisbon through the oak forests where black Iberian Pigs are bred for those famous hams. We stop at a curing plant to see how hams are processed and cured.

The process for curing Iberico Hams is different from anything any of us could have imagined. They go through a washing and drying process and then they hang them in very large wooden barns. Dry curing results in far less salt and moisture in the hams.

We toured this processing plant with the aid of a "catador." He provided us with information about the process. He said that once the hams are salted they are stored in these bodegas, (drying chambers) for up to five years. They are checked for taste and aroma often by the catadors. They are only released for sale after they meet the high standards of these professional ham tasters. Orders for the highest quality must be placed years in advance.

If I leave ham out a couple hours I worry about how safe it is to eat it. Being stored for five years is hard to comprehend. They allowed us to taste the ham and it was excellent. I guess you just have to know what you're doing!

Tonight we arrive at the Hotel Altis Grand in Lisbon, our home for the next two nights. The group is on its own for dinner tonight.

This day begins with a guided city tour that encompasses all the important landmarks of Lisbon. Our tour was on a tram small enough to travel through the very small alleys and the largest city streets. A favorite stop of Mary's and mine was a patisserie, where some of the finest pastries are created every day.

Brad, our guide, throughout the trip had from time to time treated the group with local treats. Today he treated us to the famous Pasteis de Belem. This pastry is a Portuguese egg custard tart that is made from a recipe handed down from an ancient Monastery. To be honest, it's almost worth the trip just to have this dessert. It's that good!

Belem Tower is a favorite photo stop for tourists. Originally it was built in the middle of the river but is now high and dry on the river bank. In middle ages it was the place where many famous explorers began their journeys.

We leave Lisbon this morning to visit one of the most holy and religious sites of the twentieth century. Fatima was where Lucia Santos and her cousins, Jacinta and Francisco Marto, first observed visions of the Virgin Mary around noon on May 13, 1917. This occurred on the 13th of each month through October with the exception of August. On the 13th of August they were arrested by authorities trying to extort the meanings of three secrets left with them. The children did not reveal the secrets to their captors and were released. In August it is said they saw the vision of the Virgin on the 19th of August near Valinhos.

Much is written about the secrets. Visions of Hell, and the prediction of World War II were the first two.

The third was written and was not to be opened until 1960. Two conclusions differ. One reported chaos in the catholic church and another suggests it predicted the attempted assassination of Pope John Paul 11 in 1981.

Pilgrimages are made by people all over the world the year round but especially between May and October. A small chapel has been constructed on the exact spot where it is believed the children saw the vision of Mary. A large square and Basilica were also constructed and contain two of the children's remains, Francisco and Jacinta Marto. The Catholic Church beatified them in 1970. The third became a Nun and passed in 2005.

Being here in September, we observed several people making the final portion of the Pilgrimage on their hands and knees. It was a very moving experience.

We cross back into Spain on our way to Salamanca and our Hotel Alameda Palace. On arrival in Salamanca we picked up a local tour guide and we had a guided city tour. Salamanca is noted for several important things; their golden stone buildings, the Puente Romano Bridge across the River Tomes, and it is a major educational center of Spain with several very important universities.

Dining Al Fresco, outdoors, is very popular in Europe. Our group enjoyed it every chance we could and our night in Salamanca was another very good experience. This group was a group that many had traveled together often and enjoyed having large gatherings for dinner. Most of the group ate dinner under the shadow of the university's great bell tower where we discussed the miracles of Fatima and the other day's activities.

Our last full day begins by driving through the rugged hills on the way to Avila. Avila is a completely walled city. The walls date back to the 11th century, with construction beginning in 1090 AD. We visited the Cathedral of Avila and the Basilica of St. Vicente. Both are very nice and rich in history.

We arrive back in Madrid for our first opportunity to do a city tour. We pick up a local expert for the tour. We visit the statue of Don Quixote in the Plaza of Espana, the Royal Palace, the Parliament Building before being dropped at our restaurant where we will have our Celebration Dinner at the Restauranti Marisqueria.

This is not a fancy restaurant. Rows of wooden tables with wooden benches. We took seats with our friends

Gary and Lynda. There are three musicians. Squeeze box, violin and percussion. They kept a lively performance the entire evening. How they kept the energy up for the entire evening is beyond me.

The food was served family style and if a platter or bowl began to get low another took its place at once. We were introduced to GREEN WINE! From what I understand it originated in Spain and that is the only place where you can purchase authentic GREEN WINE.

What I said about the food supply never lacking went double for the GREEN WINE supply. Several carafes were sprinkled on every table. We had a very attentive young lady whose only job for the evening was to watch the supply of GREEN WINE on our table. I must say she did an excellent job!

This celebration dinner, with all the energetic entertainment, the wonderful and plentiful food along with the GREEN WINE made for one of the most memorable final dinners for a tour we've ever experienced.

Brad was finally able to pry us loose for our trip back to the hotel. We had a walk of about a block to a pier where we would take a ferry across the Rio Manzanares to where our motor coach was waiting to return the group to the hotel.

Over the years we've been fortunate to have some of the best tour guides in the business. Vicky in China, Tarek in Egypt and on this tour we found another top-notch tour guide, Bradley Dick! Thank you Brad for an outstanding trip to Spain and Portugal.

Our return flight was direct from Madrid to Chicago leaving at 11:50 A.M. We were grateful we did not have an early morning departure, especially after an evening with all that GREEN WINE! We arrived in Chicago at 2:15 P.M. Our flight back to Moline did not leave until 8:05 P.M.

By the time our group retrieved their luggage, cleared immigration, customs and had dinner, the time passed quickly. We returned home with many wonderful memories after having many fun times with our good friends.

Dick & Mary
Spain & Portugal

# Galapagos & Machu Picchu

A trip to either Galapagos or Machu Picchu by itself would be a true bucket list trip. Mary was firm that if we were to go that far we needed to combine those two destinations and she was absolutely correct!

We researched several companies that provided similar itineraries. Our friends at Globus worked with us through their Monograms division to customize a fifteen day trip that provided everything we wanted to see and do. The price was right and our group of ten very good friends flew to Quito, Ecuador to begin this fabulous adventure on January 22nd. We return fifteen days later on February 5.

Our group departed from Chicago a little after noon and flew to Houston, arriving at 3:30 P.M. We had a two hour layover and departed for Quito at 5:30 P.M. It was midnight when we met our local guide after clearing immigration in Quito. We were off to the hotel for a very short night's rest prior to our city tour.

Quito, Ecuador is the capital city and has an altitude of 9,350 feet. We had been advised most of the land portion would be at this height, or above, all the way to 11,152 at Machu Picchu. Many people advised altitude sickness might be an issue because we are only about 700 feet in altitude where we live.

The City Tour was impressive. There is much history about the Incas and Spaniards. Independence Square, the formidable Cathedral, and Basilica with such beautiful stained glass is a memory of Quito you will not forget.

We boarded a charter flight the next morning for Baltra in the Galapagos. Immediately, we transferred to Santa Cruz Island where we boarded our ship, the *Santa Cruz II*. This Expedition cruise ship is a very modern vessel. It has fifty cabins on three decks. It contains indoor and outdoor dining, library, fitness room, hot tub, elegant bar and lounge. We are traveling in comfort for the next four nights!

Each Galapagos Island is unique because there is wildlife found only on that specific island and no place else in the world. The topography of each island is also quite varied. We did visit six islands in five days.

To visit the islands we would load from the ship into Panga Boats. Panga Boats are rubber boats with a small outboard motor and they hold about ten people. There are no docks on the islands and the Pangas were ideal to nose onto sandy beaches for us to unload and hike the trails.

Before our first island visit we had a meeting in the lounge and were given strict instructions about what is allowed and not allowed while ashore. Under no circumstances could anyone touch or attempt to touch any animal, bird or turtle. If they are encountered on a trail they have the right of way and you must get out of their way without any hassle to them. We must stay on the natural paths and not walk off of them. Everyone must stay close to our expedition guides and not go off on our own.

In addition to the varied wildlife, the beaches were quite different. Baltra had the white sand, Santiago Island had the black sand and Rabida had the red beaches. We had a Panga excursion where we could view the scenic cliffs of Genovesa, Island. This was the most difficult island to hike because Prince Phillip's Steps were steep and hazardous. They did lead to sightings of the blue-footed boobies and masked boobies. By the way, boobies are birds!

We had a visit to a rescue hospital for the East Pacific green sea turtle where we saw turtles well over a hundred years old that were larger than we could have imagined without seeing them. This rescue facility would also nurse back to health injured turtles and release them back into the wild.

A trip to the Galapagos will give you the opportunity to view the most unique and varied wildlife of any place in the world. It is well worth the time and expense to travel to these well-protected islands. It is a destination that should be visited as we did off a small ship for several days. One day from a large cruise ship cannot educate you to the true experience of the Galapagos.

Our final day was a cruise to San Cristobal Island which Charles Darwin first visited in 1835. Several species are endemic to this island. The Chatham mockingbird and the Chatham lava lizard are two that are not found elsewhere in the Galapagos or the world.

After lunch we flew on our charter to Quito and then on to Lima, Peru and our hotel, the Allpa Hotel and

Suites. We had time to rest about an hour and our group went to dinner.

In my younger years I had served as President and Chairman of the Board of two Banks. I knew how important it is to notify your credit card company of your travel plans. I called my Chase Bank card and my US Bank card. The customer care people gave very different responses to me.

Chase thanked me for letting them know and said we should have no problems since I had called them. The US Bank person advised me they would more than likely at some point decline the card as I traveled and I would then have to call them to confirm it is me and they would reopen the account. They told me this was standard procedure for foreign travel. I asked for a supervisor and explained I would be in very remote areas of Ecuador and Peru and I more than likely would not have access to phones. This was before international cell phone plans were readily available in those areas. I told them not to decline the card. If it was used it most certainly would be me using it. The supervisor thanked me and said she would flag the account so it would not be a problem.

We left our hotel with our group and had a very nice dinner. I had used the US Bank card a couple times in Quito and had no problem. I presented it in Lima at the restaurant and of course it was declined! My friends were almost rolling on the floor. They were having a really good time making sport of my issue. The Chase card came through for the balance of the trip. I of course was furious.

When we do groups like this we always include a city tour when we can. The next day we toured Lima. Lima is a city of over nine million people. They must all drive at the same time. Our group decided we had never experienced traffic jams like we saw in Lima. At large intersections, cars would face each other bumper to bumper and no one could move. There were few traffic lights. Driving in Lima was simply insane!

We did enjoy the city. Of course these City Tours have their share of Cathedrals and Basilicas. They are rich in Spanish history and we went to the Cathedral where we viewed the sealed wooden coffin containing the remains of Francisco Pizarro in the lower level burial crypts. Pizarro was an important Spanish explorer in Peru's history.

Next morning we flew from Lima to Cusco, Peru. An important stop in Cusco was the Santo Domingo Monastery. Formerly it was referred to as, "The Golden Temple". It was built to worship the Sun and its walls were covered with sheets of gold. When the Spanish conquered the Incas, the walls and precious gold and silver items were used as a ransom for the Inca Chief Atahualpa. Spanish settlers tore down the temple but used the foundation to build the Santo Domingo Monastery.

We moved from Cusco to the highest part of the trip on our way to the Valley of the Kings. The amphitheater at Sacsayhuaman is 12,211 feet. It was difficult to move about at this altitude. Being a runner I knew of a product called Breathe Right Strips. They fit over the bridge of your nose and they do open the nasal passages and allow you an additional fifteen or twenty percent more air. They were very helpful at this altitude. None of our people had suffered the altitude sickness we had been warned about at this point.

Driving into the settlement of Urubamba in the Valley of the Kings where our hotel was located was not impressive. However our hotel, Sonesta Posadas Del

Inca Yucay turned out to be most impressive. Originally it was built to be a Monastery but was converted to an eighty-seven-room hotel. The grounds were beautiful and had many flowering bushes and plants. The surrounding mountains were beautiful. It was a perfect location. It was an awesome sight when we saw llamas strolling the grounds of the hotel not paying any attention to anyone around them. We knew this hotel would be very good.

We were met as soon as we got out of our vehicles by two very nice young ladies dressed in authentic Inca dresses and asked to move to a private conference room for our check-in and complimentary welcome drink.

One of the fellows in our group who was almost my age kept referring to me as his "Dad." He was kidding about me to the ladies and joking how I was the oldest person in the group. These hotel customer care personnel speak perfect English in most cases. However, I was the only person in our group that speaks Spanish. I said to the ladies, "El Hombre es mi Abuelo! Hoy es un cumpleano. Es mi Abuelo's cien cumpleano."

I told them, "This man is my grandfather and today is his 100th birthday." They provided more complimentary drinks and left us for a few minutes. Upon return they came into the room with a birthday cake with candles, singing happy birthday. It didn't have a hundred candles but the check-in turned out to be a great time had by all. It is significant to note, he did not call me dad again on that trip.

*Dick & Mary at Valley of the Kings*

Early next morning, we boarded a train for Machu Picchu, the "Lost City of the Incas." through the Sacred Valley of the Kings. The train ride through the mountains was a spectacular sight. In some ways it reminds you of our own Rocky Mountains. It was a short ride, about fifty miles and only a couple hours.

We arrived in Agues Calientes, also known as Machu Picchu Pueblo, mid-morning and were transported by motor coach directly up to Machu Picchu via one of the narrowest and most curving roads Mary and I've ever experienced. I was sitting on the seat by the window. Looking down from my window, it actually appeared that I was out over the edge of the road looking down for thousands of feet! Large buses were coming down the same road at very fast speeds. The ride up to, as well as down from Machu Picchu was a thrilling experience. I'm truly surprised there are not several accidents each year on that road. We were assured these drivers are very experienced and accidents are very rare. Okay, it's best if you close your eyes!

We presented our vouchers and received our tickets. When you travel as often and to as many places as Mary and I do, it is very difficult to have a really big WOW moment. Leaving the ticket area you walk through a tree lined pathway for a couple hundred feet. When you reach the end of the pathway you come out into a wide open space very high up and have the most panoramic view of Machu Picchu.

*Machu Picchu*

This was a true WOW experience. Having seen this exact view of Machu Picchu in books and magazines for years, the feeling of actually being here was a moving experience. I confess to having tears running down my face. It was that emotional of an experience. Every time I see pictures of Machu Picchu I remember the deep feelings I experienced with the first view we had of this amazing sight.

When you see in person the size of Machu Picchu it's easy to understand why it took almost forty years to complete. Emperor Pachacuti was said to have had it built as an estate for himself. How they were able to construct something that size out of such huge stones with the equipment they had is an amazing feat.

Our group had a prearranged time to meet for our return to the city below. This time I sat on the mountain side so I wouldn't have to look over the edges!

Our hotel was the El Mapi. It was a hotel located on the main street downtown. We went inside to register and it was very dark in the reception area. I couldn't see very well and asked them to turn on a light so I could sign the register. A man with a cell phone shined it on my papers.

We were on the fourth floor and were told we had to walk since the elevator was not working at the time. Bellmen would bring our luggage in a few minutes. As we walked up to our room there were candles in glass holders on the stair steps about every third step. Our room had several candles in glass but sadly no electricity.

No mention was made as we registered about no

power. I went back to the front desk and inquired. They told me a storm the night before had knocked out power throughout much of the city. We felt very uncomfortable because we felt that many candles with open flames represented a very real fire hazard.

Our group met in the lobby to discuss dinner. The hotel restaurant said they could provide sandwiches and food that did not require cooking. We decided since the rest of the area had no power we may as well stay here and do what we had to do. We were told they did have plenty of drinks and beers.

No more had we sat down and been introduced to our server when the power came back on. It was greeted with a rousing cheer. Since the power was back we were told if we were patient we could have pretty much what we wanted off the menu. The meal turned out to be very good and we relaxed as all the candles on the stairs and throughout the hotel were extinguished.

The next day we took the train back to Cusco and flew back to Lima. We arrived in Lima mid-afternoon and had a hotel until late evening. We transferred to the airport for a flight at 1:10 A.M. from Lima to Houston.

We arrived back in Houston at 6:40 A.M. We had two hours between flights, leaving Houston at 8:50 A.M. returning to Chicago at 11:30 A.M.

I know you're wondering what I did about the credit card issue. I did not rest until I was able to speak in person with the President of US Bank. We worked together. He sent me a letter of apology and he advised that my issue resulted in a change of policy on how they treat international travelers.

Mary and I rate this trip as one of our top five favorite trips. It was an incredible experience that we would recommend to everyone.

# Tahiti

People ask us when they find out we travel the world. "What is the favorite place you've been?" Mary and I agreed long ago it is Tahiti.

The flight to Papeete is almost a nine hour flight from Los Angeles. Some of our group felt it would be a much easier trip if they would fly to Los Angeles and overnight in a hotel before making that long flight to Papeete. Actually, that is the way to do it.

Mary and I along with some of the group left Moline on a 6:00 A.M. flight to Chicago. We had an 8:00 A.M. flight to Los Angeles, arriving just prior to 11:00 A.M. LA time. We met those that had traveled the day before and immediately boarded the noon flight to Papeete.

By the time we boarded the flight to Papeete we had already been traveling for almost twelve hours and we had another nine hours ahead of us.

We would be at the Sofitel Tahiti Maeva Beach for two nights before boarding our cruise ship.

We arrived in Papeete, claimed our luggage, and cleared immigration and customs. We took the hotel transfer to the Sofitel and checked in. The group decided to meet for dinner thirty minutes after we checked in.

In the room, Mary looked at me and said, "Let's not do dinner tonight." I was fine with that. We didn't even unpack the luggage, we went directly to bed.

By morning we were good and met the group for breakfast. Our friends Lane and Joyce asked if we'd like to join them and we did. They are very successful farm people and have been around farm animals all their lives. The same with me. I had been raised on the farm for a while growing up and had many pet farm animals. Mary did not have any experience with animals of any kind. She did not have pets as a child.

The restaurant area of the five star Sofitel was open on three walls. We had a table close to the open area. Everyone was fascinated to see chickens, roosters and exotic birds allowed to roam freely on the grounds. All was going well until all four of us went to get our food from the breakfast buffet.

Chickens are very smart animals. When they're left to roam free around people, they become tame and are not afraid of humans. They also know when no one is at the table that's their opportunity to fill their craws. Mary and I had just returned to the table and were in the process of being seated when one of the chickens hopped right up on the table next to Mary and took a big bite of a piece of toast.

Her scream is still etched into my memory. If you've never been around animals, that can be quite frightening. Of course the three of us laughed after we had calmed her down. When we go to dinner with Lane and Joyce even now, there are times when the chicken story comes up.

Our ship overnights in Papeete. Because many flights arrive late evening passengers can board around noon but the ship does not leave until five P.M. the next day. This does allow everyone to explore Tahiti during the next day if you did not arrive early like our group.

We are to sail to the islands of Moorea, Taha'a, Rarotonga, Bora Bora, Huahine and Rangiroa.

Quite honestly the reason we like to travel here is not because of the many different things to do. The South Pacific is simply the most beautiful part of this entire planet.

Our cabin was a balcony cabin facing forward directly under the bridge. This cabin's location was the most interesting I believe we've ever experienced. As we entered each port we could view exactly what the Captain was viewing.

When arrival in port was a morning arrival, we would order breakfast from room service. Having breakfast while sitting on our balcony and viewing some of the most beautiful scenery in the world is something you will never forget. Every port was a picture postcard experience. On the hillsides you would see multi-million dollar estates with fantastic ocean views. The ports in the South Pacific are clean even though they have commercial operations. They are direct opposite of what you see in the Caribbean in industrial ports. Our cabin location was perfect for this part of the world.

The first stop was Moorea, only eleven miles Northwest of Papeete but we cruised all night and arrived around 8:00 A.M. The most memorable thing about Moorea was the beautiful scenery.

Rarotonga has the French Polynesian airport and has more population and tourist appeal. Scuba diving and snorkeling attract many visitors each year. The ocean floor is almost 13,000 feet below sea level and is one of the deepest places on earth.

Huahine was an interesting port. We did an island tour that provided awesome scenery from mountainous overlooks and included a boat tour out to a pearl farm. We had a small group visit the little pearl farm and pottery shop constructed on pilings sunk in the ocean floor. We were able to learn about how these oyster craftsmen would insert what they called a nucleus into the oysters that will eventually grow into a pearl. The women loved this because they could purchase pearls that were either mounted or unmounted. Also available here were pieces of handmade pottery.

Rangiroa is an island where there really is not much to do except scuba and snorkel. There are only a few thousand people that live here. It is said the diving and snorkeling is some of the best in the world and our stop here was mostly to accommodate guests on the ship for that opportunity.

Bora Bora is probably the island you hear most about. During World War II the United States used Bora Bora as a major supply base. The military improvements such as the airport constructed in World War II have bolstered the tourist business.

It was James Michener who wrote the book *Tales of the South Pacific* just after the war in 1946 and Rodgers and Hammerstein who turned the book into the musical *South Pacific* in 1949 and the movie in 1958 that popularized Bora Bora and the colorful character, Bloody Mary. No visit to Bora Bora is a success unless you find your way to Bloody Mary's and have a Bloody Mary, or maybe two. The stop here was really a fun stop, you just don't want to miss it.

The first over water bungalows were introduced to the Tahitian islands in 1967 at the Bali Hai Hotel in Raiatea as simple rooms over water. Bora Bora now has some of the most famous in the world. They have evolved from simple rooms over water to luxurious suites that rival any five star hotel room anywhere. The cruise ship did overnight in Bora Bora to allow passengers to enjoy the water bungalow experience.

If you travel enough you will look back and remember something you should have done, but you just didn't do. The water bungalows in Bora Bora fall into that category for us. If and when we return they will be a top priority for us.

Back in Papeete we disembark the ship and had purchased a half day stay at the hotel to pass the day. Our flight back to Los Angeles would depart at 9:30 P.M. Tahiti time and arrive 8:30 A.M. Los Angeles time.

When you arrive back into the States at Los Angeles International you must claim your luggage, clear immigration and customs and then re-check the luggage to its final destination.

Many of our people had received their luggage and we were having a good laugh because somebody's luggage had broken open and the contents were all over the luggage belt. Ladies' unmentionables, dresses and just about everything was on the carousel. You guessed it! The unmentionables belonged to one of the ladies in our group.

Our friend collected her belongings, put them in the suitcase only to find the zipper was destroyed and there was no way to close the case. We took her luggage to the Air Tahiti luggage attendant, and we filed a claim for damage. Obviously this had happened before because the attendant says, "No worries." She produced a very large roll of duct tape, the suitcase was securely taped and all was good for the balance of the trip.

If you want to see the most beautiful places on planet Earth, find your way to Tahiti and the South Pacific.

# Carnival Paradise Inaugural

As I've mentioned before, being invited to an inaugural cruise is such an honor. No matter how many you're invited to, it is very difficult not to be thrilled and excited.

Many times invitations like that come to our office and are very specific to limit the invitation to one agent per agency. Never in all our years in business have we traveled unless it included both of us. We simply decline them. Or, we say we'll attend if it includes both of us. That works sometimes.

In this case the invitation to attend the inaugural sailing for the Carnival Paradise did include both of us and we were excited to accept it. I called our Carnival Rep and thanked him for the invite. These invitations come three or four months before the event. Our Rep was in our office a couple times and we talked often between the receipt of the invitation and the cruise.

We always advise our clients to fly down to a cruise at least one day prior to sailing. We took our own advice and flew to Miami the day before the inaugural of the *Paradise*.

There are always executives of the cruise line, lots of press and important agents aboard. Mary and I both like to dress well, so we had packed her nicest gowns and my tux and headed off to Miami.

People that know me well know that I am always early for everything. When we lead groups I tell our clients, "Early is good. Nothing bad happens when you're early." In fact one of our nice clients, Lynda, made me a T-shirt with that saying silk screened on the front.

We arrived to the pier early. Ship was to sail at 5:00 P.M. but we arrived at noon. Most cruise lines expect passengers to board between 1:00 P.M. and 4:00 P.M. About 12:30 P.M. they began to check passengers in and send them to a holding area until the ship was ready to board passengers.

Mary and I presented ourselves at the counter with luggage and passports in hand. To our surprise, neither of us were on the passenger manifest!

I had talked with our Rep a few days prior to leaving and had asked about documents and he told me no documents are issued for an inaugural. Our names would be on the official manifest. "Not to worry!" Make a memo to yourself. When someone tells you, "Not to worry," it is really time to worry!

We had created a file with the invitation, all letters and my personal notes about the cruise. I presented my file to a supervisor that had been called to help our reservation clerk with our sticky situation.

She may have not wanted a scene around other passengers that were checking in. Very pleasantly and quietly, she said, "Please bring your luggage and come with me." We were introduced to the "Problem room." We really didn't know there was such a thing as the "Problem room." Now we do.

The "Problem", she explained, is that Rep does not work for Carnival any longer. And, he did not provide any paperwork indicating he had invited us for this cruise. Inaugural cruises usually sail at full capacity and she advised this was no exception.

Time moved slowly for us. The supervisor had left us in the "Problem Room" while she "looked into what I can do." We were in a pickle because our flights home were after the cruise returned and we did not have any hotel reservations if we did not cruise.

It seemed like forever when the supervisor returned, handed us our passports and said, "Welcome aboard!" We thanked her over and over for her assistance.

We boarded the ship shortly before it sailed and were shown to our cabin. The surprise we had when we opened the door was unreal. Our cabin turned out to be a suite complete with a lovely balcony.

All Carnival personnel were professional, pleasant and worked very hard to resolve the issue. There just wasn't any way to thank all of them enough.

# Magical China, Yangtze River & Hong Kong

Usually we try to do something interesting for prospective clients when Mary and I feel we have a "special trip offering." It was early in May and we mailed an invitation to several of our good friends and clients to enjoy a Chinese dinner with us. We had found an exciting fifteen day itinerary to China that could include a three day optional extension to Hong Kong.

A representative of Avalon Waterways would be presenting a slide show featuring the principal areas the group would visit. Eighteen accepted the invitation. Laura, a sales manager from Avalon made one of the best presentations we had ever seen! Seventeen of the people attending that night booked the trip. Eight of them before we left the room!

If you're planning a trip to China, start the visa process very early. Getting a visa to enter China is a time-consuming and intensive process. One blank space on the application, or one answer they don't like will send it back to you for completion, additional information, or possibly, denial of entry. We used a professional visa service for the group and it was well worth the cost and reduced the time it took to get everyone their visa.

Our trip to China is scheduled for September 4th through September 19th. It will include some of the most interesting attractions around the country requiring many inter-China flights as well as a cruise on the Yangtze River and the extension to Hong Kong.

Documents for the group arrived in our office on August 10th and we invited the group to our home for a cookout with brats and burgers around our in-ground pool on Sunday, August 12th. This turned out to be a great ice breaker. Although several in the group had traveled together before, it was a good way to build excitement for the trip and acquaint everyone.

On September 4th we boarded a 5:22 A.M. flight, Moline to Chicago, arriving there at 6:15 A.M. We took the early flight because if there was a problem or cancellation on the flight we had options. Missing the flight to Beijing would delay us at least a day and ruin a great deal of the trip.

Our connecting flight to Beijing departed at 11:56 A.M. for a twelve hour and forty four minute flight. With the twelve hour time difference, we arrived in Beijing about 1 P.M. their time.

Upon arrival in Beijing we had to walk a considerable distance from our gate to the passport control area. It went fairly quick after we presented our passports and we were cleared to enter the general population of China.

Our guide, Vickie, would be with us for the entire trip except for the Hong Kong extension. She was waiting for us with our group's name on a sign. Honestly she looked like a teenager, but she would turn out to be an outstanding guide. We were taken directly to the Westin Hotel that would be our home for the next four nights at about 4 P.M. Beijing time.

Most of our group wanted to stay awake so we could acclimate to the different time zone. Staying awake till our bedtime hour would help reset our body clocks. Nothing was planned for the rest of the day so our group decided to walk around the city close to our hotel.

When dinner time came we asked the concierge about a good place to eat that could accommodate our group. He gave us the name of a restaurant in the mall about a block from the hotel. He made a reservation for us.

It immediately became clear that language would be an issue on this trip. The group was ushered into a large private room. In the center was a circular table large enough to hold all of us. In the center of the table was a Lazy Susan.

We asked for menus in English. Even though they were in English they were difficult to read because the entrees were Chinese and the pricing was in the Chinese currency. Our servers took our orders. We ordered a considerable variety of food. We made it clear each couple wanted separate bills for the meal. They shook their heads in full understanding and all was going well.

The food arrived. To our surprise they put every dish on the Lazy Susan without any instruction as to who had ordered it or what it was.

That was okay with the group. It had to be. We spun the Lazy Susan and helped ourselves to whatever we could reach. It was fun. Everyone enjoyed being able to try the many different choices.

Finally the bill arrived! Yes, I said THE bill. It was one giant bill for the entire group. Everyone's drinks, and dinner entrees were all lumped together. Because I was the leader of the group, they presented me the bill. The whole group was laughing their heads off and perfectly happy to let me pay the bill.

Not so my traveling friends. I called for the menu again. Passed it around and said, "Figure out what you think you owe and give it to me." Fortunately, everyone had located ATMs and had gotten the Chinese yuan.

A large stack of bills materialized in front of me. After counting a couple of times it was clear I was a considerable amount short! I passed the menu around the table again reminding everyone, to "Pony up" and to be sure to include the gratuity. After the next count we determined we had the correct amount, or a least close to it. Everybody teased me about how disappointed they were that I didn't treat them for the meal. It was pretty clear this was going to be a very long trip if we go through this every meal.

Breakfasts are favorites of ours when we travel. They were all included in the price of our trip. The Westin Hotel had a very good breakfast buffet menu. There was a good selection of fruits and veggies for our vegan friends. You could choose items making a very good American style breakfast or they had items for the local Chinese guests.

We will be spending a good deal of time today at Lama Temple. This Temple is called the "Palace of Peace and Harmony." It is a temple and a monastery of Tibetan Buddhism. It is one of the largest temples in China proper. It was built with a combination of Chinese and Tibetan architecture. It was very nice to wander the large halls and courtyards observing the beautiful art and statues.

As we approached the entrance the smell of incense was so overpowering we could barely breathe. Inside the first courtyard were huge barrels and open fires that would remind you of BBQ grills back home, all burning incense. All the locals were carrying big sticks of incense.

After the visit to the temple we had a short walk to a Hutong. This was a very interesting walk. A Hutong is a very narrow street or alley lined on each side by what looks like very small and shabby dwellings. Our guide, Vickie, had arranged for us to visit one of the homes along this Hutong.

What a surprise! We were met by a very gracious host dressed in a beautiful silk dress with ornate embroidery. It is courteous to remove shoes when visiting a home. We left them in the area just inside the door.

From the outside this home looked very small and not so well maintained. Each home shared common walls and were connected together. No grass in sight along this very narrow street that was no more than twenty feet wide.

After removing our shoes we could not believe the beauty and the size of this home. It is completely deceiving from the outside. It turned out the home was constructed in a square around a quite large open courtyard inside. The home was very modern. The kitchen had all the current appliances, a living room with a nice sized television, and immaculate bedrooms.

From the outside you would never believe you would find the comfort and beauty of this home. It is easy to believe we were taken to one of the better homes but it was a very impressive way to begin our trip to China.

Vickie told us the next day would be a long day. The day would include visits to Tiananmen Square, The Forbidden City, The Imperial Palace, and Summer Palace. We would finish the day with the signature Peking Duck Dinner.

On our motor coach between leaving the Westin Hotel and arriving at Tiananmen Square, Vickie was very serious and asked for our complete attention. She told us when we're on the motor coach she will answer any question regarding Tiananmen Square and anything that has happened there. However, she asked us not to ask any questions at all of her while we are off the coach at Tiananmen Square.

According to her, the Square is filled with Communist Secret Agents that move among the crowd. They listen to everything and everybody. We were told to keep any critical comments to ourselves for discussion later on the motor coach. Many tourists have been arrested for unfavorable comments or actions here.

She also told us we might experience some very strange requests from the locals. Specifically, many like to have their pictures taken with American tourists and not to be surprised if you're asked to pose with the locals.

Mary and her sister Marcy are identical twins and are very tall by Chinese standards. They were constantly being asked for pictures. The Chinese didn't want me in the picture, they wanted me to take the picture!

We entered the Forbidden City and were amazed at the size. It was built in fourteen years. From 1406 to 1420. There are 980 buildings with 8700 rooms. It is completely surrounded by a thirty-foot high wall and a moat. For almost five hundred years it was the Imperial Palace of China and the home of twenty four Emperors. It is the largest palace in the world!

The day finished at the Summer Palace. This had a beautiful setting on a very large lake and was the summer home of several Emperors. After seeing this and the Forbidden City we realized the Chinese Emperors really knew how to live!

Most of our friends were looking forward to the Peking Duck Dinner. This is supposed to be the greatest meal since sliced bread. To be very honest, it was just okay, not great. However, to be fair about it we don't care for duck. Our group pretty much felt the same. The dinner was just okay but how many can say they experienced a Peking Duck Dinner in Beijing!

Vickie told us we would be leaving the hotel about 7:30 A.M. tomorrow. She said most of the tours would leave about 8:00 A.M. for the Great Wall but by leaving early we would have a great walk on the wall without many other tourists and visitors in our way. We took great pictures of the wall without people in them.

**Great Wall of China**

Vickie was indeed correct. We arrived very early and had a short wait before we could enter through the gates and walk on the Wall. The Great Wall of China is for certain another thing you just have to see to believe.

When you climb the steps and walk out on the Wall, you look to your right and to the left. It just goes forever. Actually it is over 2,500 miles in length. It really takes your breath away when you realize exactly where you are standing.

Many questions come to mind when you consider much of this was built seven centuries before Christ! Our guide explained the Chinese were far advanced in the art of wall building. They used materials close to the portions they were building and it was very difficult and hard labor. Vickie told us no records were kept but it is estimated that hundreds of thousands of Chinese laborers perished in the building of the wall.

We were given a good amount of time to spend on the wall. Every minute we were there, the crowd multiplied. By the time we left it was wall-to-wall people on the Wall!

All of the group was beginning to see the value of such a knowledgeable guide.

Next was the Sacred Way of Ming Tombs. This sacred area has tombs of several Emperors along a beautiful walkway. Statues of animals line the pathway and it is a beautiful walk. We only had time to walk a small part of it. It is a 4.5 mile walk from beginning to end. It would be a nine mile round trip that was just too far for the time allotted to the visit.

Vickie had us up early for breakfast. Our luggage was sent ahead of us to the airport. We were treated to a very interesting and fun Rickshaw ride through some very ancient areas and more Hutongs of Beijing. After the Rickshaw ride we were motor coached to the airport for our China Eastern 2 P.M. flight to Xian. The evening was on our own for dinner.

Another early morning for us. Vickie explained on the ride from the airport to our hotel in Xian our first stop tomorrow would be the Terracotta Warriors. It would be very important to be one of the first groups to arrive. Because it was so important to be early she set our departure time a half hour sooner than other groups in our hotel.

We arrived at the Terracotta Warriors site before any other tour buses. It was raining quite hard. The parking lot was a long walk, almost a quarter mile, but our coach drove almost to the entrance and let us off. Our group was the very first group inside and we were able to take pictures without being hassled and were able to move about easily.

*Terracotta Warriors*

This too is a must see exhibit. It is estimated there are between six thousand and eight thousand clay statues of life sized soldiers, horses and chariots in battle formations. No two are alike. Much is still buried but excavation has continued since 1974. Historians believe they date back as far as 259 BC and were created to protect Emperor Qin's military power in his afterlife.

Lunch today included a demonstration of noodle making that was truly impressive. For several minutes a waiter worked the noodle dough, folding and refolding it. What made it so impressive was after all the working with the dough he threw it forcefully onto the table and the dough fell into perfectly shaped lengths of noodles.

Our afternoon ended with a brief stop at the Dayan Pagoda. This is a very impressive Buddhist Temple. It is several stories tall with very winding stairs. When you make it to the top it has a spectacular view of the city. This Pagoda is a very holy place for Buddhists. The continuing rain shortened our stay but it was worth the stop.

September 11th, and today we board another flight from Xian to Chongqing. Two big things are to happen today! After landing in Chongqing during a very heavy rainstorm we were to proceed directly to the Zoo where we are to see the pandas. Then directly following the zoo visit we are to board the *Victoria Anna* for our three night cruise on the Yangtze River.

We arrive at the Zoo and find it closed! It was easy to understand because it was pouring rain. Our guide Vickie pulled out her cell phone and called someone. A few minutes later the Zoo Director arrived in person. He unlocked the gate and opened the Zoo just for our group!

He was upfront with us. He said because of the rain we might not see any pandas but we were able to walk to their area to see for ourselves. Vickie knew the way and we took our umbrellas and rain gear and walked to their area. Surprise, surprise, they were sitting in the rain eating their bamboo, just as cute as they could be. Those with cameras got some excellent pictures even though it was such lousy weather.

None of us could believe our guide Vickie, had so much clout that she could make a single phone call and get a major attraction open just for our small group. But, it actually happened! This was the only time in our itinerary where we had a chance to see the pandas and it would have been a real disappointment to miss them. Vickie saved the day.

On a very high note we are off to embark the beautiful *Victoria Anna* for our three night, four day cruise on the Yangtze River. When we first view the ship it reminds us of the river cruise ships we see on the Mississippi. This ship is much smaller. It has a passenger capacity of only 266 guests and a crew of 138. The *Victoria Anna* began sailing the Yangtze in 2006 and is luxury, pure and simple. Balcony rooms for our entire group, a swimming pool, two elegant restaurants, and amazing decor and artwork will make for a very memorable cruise on the Yangtze.

The Yangtze is the third longest river in the world traveling over 3900 miles. We will be traveling the most scenic and popular portion of the river, the Three Gorges. They are, Qutang Gorge, five miles, the Wu Gorge, twenty-seven miles and the Xiling Gorge, forty-seven miles.

Once again it was clear that Vickie was well known and an important guide in China. She told us she knew the cruise director on the *Victoria Anna* and she would be getting information about how and when to line up for the shore excursions about fifteen minutes before the other tour guides and passengers.

With that information we would line up first and get the best seating on the buses or boats if it was a water excursion. Our group was first in line every time. There is just no way to put a value on a guide like Vickie.

The stop today was at Fengdu Ghost City. There are a number of temples and shrines here dedicated to what happens in the afterlife. It is a very long hike to the top from the water level and everyone was cautioned to wear good shoes and be physically fit for the difficult climb to the top of Ming Mountain. These shrines and temples used to look down on the old town of Fengdu. However when the Three Gorges Dam was built the water level rose and submerged the city. All residents were relocated on a rebuilt version of the city on the bank directly across the river on higher ground.

Mary and I were in top physical condition since we are runners. We were definitely exhausted when we reached the top after approximately seven hundred steps. Many would climb awhile then rest, then they would climb again and repeat the process until they reached the top.

It is said you must pass three tests when you die to move onto the afterlife. Characters in costume this day were on hand to see if we were worthy to, "pass on."

Mary and I passed! The return down the steps to the ship was a great deal easier.

The morning hours the next day was scenic cruising through spectacular Wu Gorge. We stayed on the upper deck so we could take in the fantastic views on both sides of the ship.

After lunch, Vickie gathered us together so we could again be first in line to board small motorized boats for a three and a half hour trip through the very picturesque Lesser Gorges tributary. We were told not to drink any water, coffee or tea on the boat because it was not safe to drink. It was also good advice because there were no bathrooms. This was a photographer's dream and around every bend in the tributary we were given another postcard photo opportunity.

Friday, September 14th was another early morning. This trip seemed like we had a number of very early mornings but we came here to see as much as we could see. We didn't want to sleep through China. Our luggage was to be ready and outside our room for pickup by 7:45 A.M.

We docked today at Sandouping where we could get off the ship and walk around for up to three hours on the Three Gorges Dam. This is the largest water conservation project ever built. Over 1.3 million citizens had to be relocated in order to construct this dam. It created a reservoir of 400 miles in length. It was built to serve three purposes, flood control, hydroelectric power and navigation improvement. It improved barge tonnage by 500 percent. It was very interesting but we did not need the full three hours on shore. We returned to the ship after a couple hours.

After lunch we went to the airport for our short flight to Shanghai. We walked the Bund, which literally means levee or embankment. This is a great area for running and biking. We spent some time here just, "People watching." The group was to have dinner on their own. We broke the group up so we did not duplicate the Beijing dinner fiasco.

Our last day in Shanghai would be a busy one. In the morning we toured the beautiful Yu Yuan Flower Garden and a silk factory. The women all liked the silk factory and they made many purchases. After lunch we went to the Shanghai Museum and Children's Palace. All were very interesting but we're beginning to wear down.

The evening was our farewell dinner and it included one of the most physical acrobatic shows we've ever seen. We were leaving the mainland with a lot of very wonderful memories tomorrow.

Vickie takes our group to the airport. Two would fly back to Chicago. The remaining fifteen will board Hong Kong Airline's flight HX 237 at 11:55 A.M. to Hong Kong. We will say goodbye to her at the airport in Shanghai.

The night before we were to leave our guide, Vickie, I had quietly discussed her gratuity with the group. I told everyone it was their decision what to give her but I did say she was one of the better guides Mary and I ever had. I don't know how much her gratuity was but I do know it was substantial.

Everyone in our group treated Vickie as if she was a daughter or family member. Something happened at the airport that I had never seen before and have not seen since. Our group had become so attached to her that it was very difficult to say goodbye. It was tearful for us, but never have I seen a guide so attached to a group that she openly sobbed and cried big tears. Tour guides come and go but this cherub of a young lady touched all our hearts and we still think of her often.

Our flight touched down in Hong Kong at 2:25 P.M. and we transferred directly to our hotel, the St. Regis Marriott in downtown Hong Kong for the next three nights. This hotel was pure luxury and walking distance for a number of attractions.

The Concierge told us we should take in the Temple Street Night Market. It was an easy walk and it proved to be very entertaining. Night markets originated as cheap places for locals to have entertainment. The Temple Street Market had certainly diversified over time. Tent stalls were selling men's and women's clothes. There were fortune tellers, jugglers, mimes, every kind of walking around food imaginable. It was a really fun adventure.

We made the best of our first full day in Hong Kong. We took the cable car to Victoria Park for the beautiful overview of the city. There was some haze but it was a remarkable view.

Haze was an issue in every city in China. Almost every morning you would awaken to overcast skies. It always appeared it would rain but it was just smog and air pollution. A few minutes out of town things clear up. The cities were always dreary.

Mary always organizes our activities in cities where we do not have organized tours. She found a city tour that would give us a very good overview of Hong Kong. We drove through the richest part of the city, Aberdeen Village and the beautiful beaches of Repulse Bay. The tour ended with a Sampan ride in the harbor. The day ended with a sunset dinner cruise. The food was good, the sunset was beautiful and we were once again only walking distance from the St. Regis Hotel. Walking as a group at night was very safe.

Our last day Mary had found an optional tour to Lantau Island to see the giant Buddha. This huge Buddha was several stories tall and watched over the bay and the island. It was a nice boat ride and we did visit some shops before heading back to the hotel to pack and have a relaxing dinner before our flight home.

From the time we got up to the time we returned home it was thirty two hours of travel. The flight from Hong Kong to Chicago was direct but it was long, fourteen hours and thirty two minutes in the air!

This trip rates as one of our top trips. We traveled with good friends, had an amazing tour guide and we saw some of the most interesting tourist and historical sites in the world.

# Scotland

Our group consisted of an entire motor coach of forty people. Most of them had joined the group because we had advertised it as a Dick and Mary hosted group. The trip was to be a short trip beginning with an overnight flight to Glasgow and only six hotel nights in Scotland. We motor coached the group to Chicago for our direct flight to Glasgow.

A couple that has traveled with us on several trips always travels with a portable oxygen generator. The generator has a battery that has about a four hour life. She plugs into outlets during long flights or when traveling on motor coaches while on tours. We always confirm outlets are available on planes and buses. Without the oxygen generator being able to recharge the battery or plug in, it could quickly turn into a life threatening situation.

Just prior to landing in Glasgow we were told the connecting cable to the outlet had broken in half. She was not able to charge the unit and it was operating on battery power only.

We cleared immigration and met our local guide. Our group was to begin a four hour city tour leaving directly from the airport. She had used a couple hours of battery life already and would not be able to complete the city tour without running out of oxygen.

The guide and I decided a quick way to solve the issue was to send our couple by taxi to a nearby hospital. It is a medical device and it should be able to be repaired at a hospital. Just replace the cord or tape it together.

Mid-afternoon our couple found their way to our hotel. She was carrying a large oxygen cylinder. It was certainly not portable and would last only till mid-day tomorrow.

I asked what is the story on repairing their machine. The hospital told them it was an American manufactured machine and there was nothing they could do to repair it.

Our guide advised there was no way for them to continue on the trip. The rest of the trip did not have cities large enough to exchange the large oxygen cylinders. It was clear she would run out of oxygen if they continued with the group. Getting them home would also be an issue due to the length of the flights.

All afternoon our local guide worked with their home office in London to see if they could find a solution. Nothing seemed to work. The only thing that might work in order to get them home would be to contact the manufacturer in the States and fly either a new machine or repair part to Glasgow. The best they could offer was a week to get that done.

Since they could not continue on, it was decided Mary and I would stay back with them. We didn't want to split up and the tour guide was capable of handling the group. Our job would be to keep her in oxygen and figure a way to get them and us home.

Mary and I met with the group and the tour guide early the next morning. I asked our guide if we could delay the departure from Glasgow and give me some time to look for a solution at electronic stores. We were to leave at 9:00 A.M. and she said she could only give me till 10:00 A.M. and they would leave without the four of us. It was about 8:30 A.M. by then!

I took the machine and took off on a dead run looking for electronic stores. The first one I found close to the hotel did not open until 11:00 A.M. but the owner was receiving a delivery and he asked to see the machine. He said that even if he was open he did not have what we needed but there was a store about four or five blocks away that was open for business and should be able to repair it for us.

Staying at a dead run I located the store and it was open! A young man asked to help me. He said he could provide a European cord and provide an adapter that would make the machine work. I explained my urgency and he set about the repair. I kept watching the clock and realized I was running out of time.

When he finished I over paid him and did not wait for my change. I again took off at a dead run and when I arrived back at the hotel the coach was loaded and ready for departure. The four of us boarded the coach and we departed with the group. We were within a couple minutes of being left in Glasgow.

That night we stayed in a beautiful hotel in Ballachulish after viewing the Scottish scenery. Dinner was relaxing and we had the first calm minutes of this trip. If you're going to Scotland, try to book this hotel. It has impressive views of a lake surrounded by beautiful mountains.

We ended our tour in Edinburgh where we did all the usual tourist attractions including the Edinburgh Castle, Holyrood Palace, Mary's King Close and the Royal Mile.

Usually we remember our trips by what we've seen. This trip we remember by what we almost did not see. All in all it was an excellent trip.

# Christmas Market Cruise

It was a year when the family Christmas activities would allow us the time to take a cruise on the Mississippi from Memphis to New Orleans during the Christmas week.

The American Queen Steamboat Company offered a travel agent rate for this holiday cruise. Discounted rates for holiday cruises are unheard of. We found if we booked a cabin under my name and one under Mary's name we would be able to take Mary's twin sister with us also for a travel agent rate. Mary and I would share and Marcy would have her own cabin.

We rented a car and drove to Memphis where we would drop the car and board the ship. Our first night with *The American Queen* was at the Sheraton Memphis Downtown for Sunday night. We arrived on Saturday and had booked the same hotel.

Marcy had not been to Memphis before. Of course we took her to Graceland, Beale Street and the Martin

Luther King museum before we checked in with the cruise people at the hotel on Sunday. We do not sail until 5:00 P.M. Monday.

It's interesting how the cruise line handles shore excursions. They provide a complimentary excursion in each port of call. They have their own buses that travel ahead of the ship and meet the ship at the port to transport the passengers on the excursions. They move to the next port after they finish for the day. They repeat this process each day to the end of the cruise.

Mary and I did not know what quality to expect for food and entertainment. To be honest we did not believe food would compare to the ocean cruises. What a surprise we had. The food on *The American Queen* was as good and in some cases even better than the ocean cruises.

Our first morning we had breakfast in the River Grill and Bar. Mary and her sister are quite tall. We met a delightful African American lady that most likely was not five feet tall. She was in charge of the restaurant and immediately declared they were not twins, she was a long lost triplet sister.

There was an immediate bond of friendship between the four of us. She would inquire when we might be arriving for breakfast or lunch and our table was always reserved for us, no matter how busy they were. After all, as triplets the girls were family.

The nightly entertainment was limited. A gentleman by the name of Phil Westbrook was absolutely fantastic on the piano as we waited for the dining room to open and after dinner he would play in the Captain's Lounge. The theatre was not large enough for Las Vegas style shows but they had a group of four or five singers and dancers that did a very nice job.

Our cruise was billed as a Christmas Market cruise. Vicksburg, Natchez and St. Francisville were to have Christmas Markets. All had city tours on the motor coach ending at the markets. Usually they were set up in gyms in the local high school or civic center. Honestly they were just okay. Many booths held crafts and some were not much more than a yard sale. It was still fun to meet the locals. Most of us purchased something just to help them out.

Thursday night we were docked in Natchez and it was Christmas Eve. Christmas services were offered at Methodist, Catholic and Presbyterian Churches. The ship's buses were available to take passengers to the church of their choice.

We chose a Methodist service. The Pastor was a very dynamic lady. The church was small and it was filled to capacity with locals. The service was excellent. A small choir provided excellent Christmas music and we ended with a very moving candlelight service. It was a beautiful way to celebrate Christmas Eve.

Baton Rouge was a very nice city tour even though very little was open. We stopped for a photo opportunity at the Capitol. Every time we sailed into or from a port, Phil played the calliope.

Docking at the Nottoway Plantation was very interesting because we were able to see how elegantly these antebellum plantation owners had lived in the deep South. We were separated into small groups and had a guide from the plantation for the tour. She was a fountain of statistics. According to her, there are over sixty rooms covering over 50,000 square feet of living area. This beautifully restored plantation home was built entirely by slave labor in the late 1800s.

We disembark and transfer to the airport where we fly from New Orleans to Moline, Illinois.

The story does not end here. The following August, *The American Queen* made a stop in Bettendorf at the dock by the Isle of Capri Casino. We met our friend Kim and took her to lunch at The Village Inn in Davenport. It was a great reunion and a lot of fun. On the return trip South they docked again but this time we had arranged to take fifteen of our clients and good friends aboard *The American Queen* for lunch.

Cruising the Mississippi is a luxurious experience, one you will always remember. I know we will always have fond memories of the cruise, Phil and our good friend Kim the triplet!

*Mary, Kim, Marcy*

# London, Paris & Normandy

Our good friends Daryl and Mary had been asking for this trip for a couple of years. They only wanted to go if Mary and I would travel with them. Our schedule finally allowed this trip leaving on July 12 and returning on July 20.

This would be a very short trip for what they wanted us to include in three very touristy destinations. We had dinner with Daryl and Mary and discussed the things we had enjoyed on several of our trips. We let them pick what they wanted to see based on what we told them from our personal experiences.

We developed a custom itinerary that would fit a one week time frame. Mary knew a company that specialized in customized European travel. Several days were spent tweaking it. Daryl and Mary approved the itinerary and we advertised it to our clients. A group was formed and we were on our way.

Our overnight flight to London arrived early morning. After clearing immigration and customs we were met by our transfer people and were taken directly to a very small hotel in London, the Days Inn Hyde Park. No formal activities today but the hotel told us we could purchase Hop On Hop Off tours very close to the hotel.

It turned out to be a very good way for first-time London visitors to get an idea what the city looked like. We were able to stop at the London Tower, Westminster Abbey and take a boat ride on the Thames River. It was a really good use of our time and we returned to the hotel exhausted and hungry. We had fish and chips in a little restaurant close to the hotel.

Mary had arranged a private tour to pick us up at the hotel for a trip to Bath and Stonehenge. We spent half a day touring the City of Bath and walking through the Roman Baths. Everyone picked up a sandwich to eat on the road to Stonehenge. Upon arrival at Stonehenge we were delayed for quite a while because they could not find our prepaid ticket reservations. It took us a while but we straightened things out and received the tickets. The ticket office manager threw in headsets for everyone to make up for their delay in finding our reservation.

Stonehenge has certainly changed since we were there before. A new parking lot for buses and the ticket office were moved quite a distance from the exhibit. Stonehenge ran buses back and forth but the lines were long. When we were here before you could actually walk among the rocks, touch them and be right up close. Not so anymore. They have built a circular walkway around it with stops where you could enter a number on your headset and hear the recorded message for that stop. It helped having the headset.

Morning comes and we are picked up for our private transfer to the London Rail Station where we have tickets to Paris on the Eurostar through the Chunnel under the English Channel. We traveled at almost 100 MPH and 380 feet below sea level through the Chunnel. What is so surprising is we are only in the Chunnel for about twenty minutes. It turned out it is only about thirty one miles long under the ocean.

Upon arrival in Paris we are taken to our hotel, the Hotel Astoria Astotel for two nights. Our group liked the Hop On Hop Off Tour in London and they wanted to do another one just to see as much as possible before our formal tour of Paris tomorrow.

Today is Tuesday and we have a walking tour of Paris. There is a lot of walking but we actually ride street cars, buses and take a boat ride on the Seine River.

We start the tour by arriving at the Eiffel Tower very very early. Our guide says unless you arrive early you will spend most of your time in lines and waiting for elevators at the tower. Our tickets gave us full access to the highest level of the Eiffel Tower. It is by far the best view of the city you can have in Paris.

After leaving the Tower, we were only a block from where we would board our boat for the river tour. It was interesting to view Notre Dame from this angle. It had been seriously damaged by fire in April of 2019. We got off the boat at the base of Notre Dame and were able to walk around the Cathedral and we did get some group pictures that showed it in the background. Even though the damage was severe our pictures looked pretty good. We finished the day by walking through the Latin Quarter and back to our hotel.

Mary and I have looked forward to this day. To this point, we've been everyplace the group has visited. Today we will be driving from Paris to Rouen with a stop in Giverny to visit Monet's house and gardens. Monet's gardens alone are worth the stop here. We were also able to view many of Monet's artworks inside his home.

We were supposed to visit Rouen several years before on a river cruise but we were not able to go past Giverny because of a dock strike. No problem today because we're driving. Our hotel in Rouen is the Mercure Rouen Centre. We will be here for two nights.

It was a very centrally located hotel. It was just one block off the biggest square in town. The square was lined with restaurants. All looked very good. It seemed like everyone in the group wanted to eat at a different place. That was not a problem. There were many tables set up on the square and we could all place orders and carry the food to the table. Most of the group ate at the same place. Fish and chips!

There were some veterans in our group. Of course they weren't World War II, but having been in the military they were very interested to see the various landing areas and the Normandy American Cemetery and Memorial.

Our first stop was at the Omaha Beach Museum. It was really good because we watched a film of the D Day landing on June 6, 1944. The movie was a very sobering experience. It gave us a good perspective of the size of the landing forces. It also let us feel a little of the anxiety those men had to have as they waited for their turn to advance onto the beach.

We walked Omaha Beach and Utah Beach. After having watched the movie, we realized thousands of men had perished on this very spot to preserve the freedoms all of us have today. As we walked the beach I saw a man with a T-shirt that said, "If you can read this, thank a teacher. If you can read it in English, thank a veteran." We boarded our bus to visit the Normandy American Cemetery and Memorial.

Before we arrived at the Cemetery we made a quick stop at one of the German bunkers. The bunker was well constructed and protected the German forces very well. It was easy to see why American casualties were so high.

The visit to the cemetery was a very solemn visit. It is high on a bluff overlooking Omaha Beach. There are 9,388 American soldiers buried here on these 172.5 acres. The last soldier buried here was June 19, 2018. He was Julius Pieper and was buried next to his twin brother Ludwig. We learned there is one World War I veteran Quentin Roosevelt buried next to his brother Theodore Roosevelt Jr. They are sons of former President Theodore Roosevelt. Only four women are buried here. Our guides were very well versed on the history of the cemetery.

As you walk through this immaculately manicured cemetery you notice the rows of crosses are precisely in line no matter which way you look at them.

We return to Rouen in time for dinner. We went back to the same restaurant as last night. We ate quietly as we thought about all we had learned today.

We stopped at the Palace of Versailles on the return. No tickets were purchased in advance and the day's allotment was sold out. We were able to walk the grounds and see the beautiful gardens. Maybe next time!

We stayed in Paris this night and flew back to the States the next morning. This very short trip gave everyone a good sample of London, Paris and Normandy. It was a very good time for all of us.

# Tulips & Windmills

Springtime is always a beautiful time of the year. Trees leaf out and flowers that have rested below the earth through the winter months rise up into full bloom and glorious color. This is true the world over but it is especially true in Holland.

Avalon has a river cruise called Tulips and Windmills that is only available for a very few weeks, mostly in April that showcases the beauty of Holland's tulip crop spreading beauty everyplace you look. This was especially true as our flight was descending into Schiphol Airport in Amsterdam in mid April.

Holland raises tulips as a cash crop much the same as farmers in Illinois and Iowa raise corn and beans. Mary and I had seats on the two seat side of the airplane with an unobstructed view of the land. As we were on final approach to landing we couldn't believe what we were seeing. The ground below was like a patchwork quilt of color. As far as we could see, were fields that each one must have been at least a hundred acres or larger. Each field was filled with brilliant solid colors of red, yellow, or purple. There were fields of every color of tulip grown. We knew we would see a lot of color on this trip, however to see so much before our plane had even landed was a very pleasant surprise.

Avalon met us as we exited immigration and customs with a sign with our name on it. We were transferred to a hotel close to where we would board the ship. It was still early morning but they had a staff there to check us in, collect and tag our luggage. The next time we would see our luggage would be in our cabin on the ship.

The reception area was quite nice. Complimentary coffee, tea and juices and fresh pastries were available. Since it would be a few hours before we would transfer from the hotel to the ship we could either relax in the reception area they provided or we could take a walk and explore the area close to the hotel. We took some time and enjoyed walking in the area and having a light lunch before being transferred to the ship around 3:00 P.M.

Upon arrival to the ship we were given an envelope with our room keys and we proceeded directly to our cabin. Our luggage was already in the cabin waiting for us to arrive! Avalon had provided the easiest and most pleasant process to board a cruise ship we had ever experienced.

We sailed after dinner and our first stop was Antwerp. Our local guide took us on a walking tour of the downtown area that included entrance to the Cathedral of Our Lady. According to our guide, the Cathedral began construction in 1352 AD. The largest portion being completed in 1521 AD. She claims it has never been completely finished and work continues. The church is Gothic and contains a bell tower over four hundred feet tall.

Cathedrals in Europe many times contain extremely valuable pieces of art. The Cathedral of Our Lady contains several artists' work but most famous works are by Peter Paul Rubens. "The Assumption of the Virgin Mary" is the main artwork on the altar. Other significant Rubens works are "The Raising of the Cross" and "The Descent From the Cross."

Next morning we are docked in Ghent. This day we visit Saint Bavo's Cathedral. The Gent Altarpiece, painted by Van Eyck has a great deal of interesting history. It consists of several panels. Some were removed by the Germans during World War II but were later returned. One panel "The Just Judges" was stolen sometime in the early 1930s and has never been found or returned. It does have a replacement in its place. According to our guide the church prays the original will be returned at some time in the future.

In both Middelburg and Willemstad we were treated to very nice city tours and in Willemstad we went to a farm that only raises tulips. We took some very beautiful pictures at the farm.

About a year ago Mary and I were visiting my son in Allen, Texas. As we were checking into the LaQuinta Hotel, neither of us could believe the picture that was ceiling to floor across the entire back wall behind the counter. We had taken that very picture while on the tulip farm in Willemstad! True story!

We have been anticipating the stop in Rotterdam since before we left home. Two of the most interesting shore excursions are here! The morning hours will be spent at Keukenhof Gardens and in the afternoon we tour Kinderdijk.

Mary is quite concerned as we're having breakfast. We're eating early because of the full day and our early start. The weather seems dull and overcast, no bright sunshine.

At the meeting before dinner last night the cruise director provides information about Keukenhof. It is a very large garden complex, almost eighty acres. It is only open to the public for eight weeks a year, from mid March to mid May, although private functions are held from time to time during the year.

Some of the information the cruise director gives us almost seems unreal. We're told a little over three dozen gardeners begin around the first of October planting over seven million tulip bulbs. They stagger the planting of over eight hundred varieties of tulips so they are continuously blooming for those eight weeks. The goal is to finish planting in the first week of December. It should be noted that several other flowers are used for variety such as roses, daffodils and carnations to name a few.

After breakfast we board our motor coach for Keukenhof Gardens. Mary is still concerned about the lack of sun. She must have a direct connection to the man upstairs because just as we arrived at the gardens, bright sun came out and it never left us for the remainder of the day.

I don't believe there is a way to properly describe what over seven million tulip bulbs blooming looks like. This is simply the most beautiful flower garden arrangement you will ever see. We were actually overwhelmed by what we saw. This excursion was worth the price of the entire trip by itself. Put this on your bucket list.

***Keukenhof Gardens***

We returned to the ship for a quick lunch before we head off for Kinderdijk. This works because Kinderdijk is only about ten miles from where we're docked. Our Cruise Director gave information the night before, but clearly not as much as she had for Keukenhof.

Kinderdijk is a favorite tourist site because of the numerous windmills built along a canal. Originally nineteen windmills were built here in the middle seventeen hundreds for draining local canals. Its attraction to tourists is the opportunity to photograph very good windmill pictures.

We had something happen here that we've never had happen before on any of our trips. One couple on the cruise was always late for everything. Our tour guides and those of us in the groups with them were always left waiting for them to return. They were late to board the coach off the cruise ship so we were late to begin our tour. They would go off on their own on the tours and our group would be left waiting for quite a while for them to return.

Finally in Kinderdjik, we had been sitting on the motor coach waiting for twenty minutes for this same couple to return. Our tour guide told the driver to leave. The people on the bus cheered and clapped as we pulled out of the parking lot. The ship was waiting for us to return so they could sail. We never saw them again but I would guess they found their way to the ship when we arrived the next day in Amsterdam.

We had arrived early morning and had several options to fill the day. Our last night on the ship was here in Amsterdam. On previous trips to Amsterdam we had toured the Anne Frank House, walked the red light district and had taken daytime boat trips on the canals. Mary and I decided to sign up for the romantic candle light wine and dinner cruise that evening. It was a fitting end to this wonderful trip.

Next morning we transferred to the airport for our flight home. Mary had secured the two seat side of the plane and we enjoyed seeing the fields of tulips as we departed leaving us with rich and colorful memories of tulips and windmills.

# Poland
## Warsaw, Krakow, Auschwitz, Prague

Most people would choose to visit the country of Poland later in the year than February. We boarded a direct flight on Monday, February 22 for Warsaw, the Capital of Poland. We arrived very early in the morning, around 5:00 A.M. After clearing immigration, we took a taxi directly to the hotel. Check-in time at the hotel was not until 3:00 P.M. so we decided to do some walking in the downtown area.

As we walked around we would see long lines of people at shops that were only about eight feet wide with no indoor seating. Whatever they were selling was dispensed through a door that was cut in half but closed on the bottom and opened on the top half. We call them Dutch doors in the States.

There were several shops like this as we walked about. Each one of them had lines stretching almost a block long. This seemed a little strange to us and we decided to find out about them when we returned to the hotel.

*Paczki Day in Poland*

Our concierge looked at us as if we were from a different planet. He said, "Today is Fat Tuesday!" That didn't tell either of us why there were so many lines at these little shops. He was nice however and explained Fat Tuesday in Poland is also Paczki Day. People are preparing for the fast of forty days prior to Easter and millions of Paczkis are sold in a very few hours. Consequently Fat Tuesday is also known as Paczki Day in most Polish communities.

I'll save you some trouble. Paczki is pronounced, "Poonch-key" or you could get by with "pawnch-key". Regardless of which one you choose, someone probably will try to correct how you say it.

Okay, what exactly is a Paczki? They are calorie laden Polish jelly donuts coated in powdered sugar or chocolate. They are usually only about three inches in diameter but they are packed with between four or five hundred calories. You should know they usually contain small amounts of vodka or grain alcohol! After we tried several it was no mystery why the long lines. They are absolutely delicious.

Later that evening we checked again with the concierge about a place for dinner. He honestly, but quietly, suggested we should go elsewhere besides the hotel and recommended we try, The Bulldog Pub. We did. It was quite good. They had excellent fish and chips and we each tried a tray of six different draft local beers. Each tray of beers had different beers so we enjoyed the taste of a dozen of their local craft beers. Our concierge earned his gratuity big time!

Next morning we met our tour guide. We enjoyed a walking tour of Warsaw that was very emotional and educational. Warsaw is filled with history and sadness stemming from the atrocities of World War II. We returned late afternoon to the hotel for an excellent dinner with the group. Our guide would be with us for the next five days as we travel to Krakow, Prague and Auschwitz.

It was an early morning departure. Our destination was Krakow but we were excited because we were scheduled to experience two of the top tourist attractions in Poland on the way.

Our first stop was at the Jasna Gora Monastery in Czestochowa, Poland. We would be seeing the Black Madonna of Czestochowa, also known as Our Lady of Czestochowa.

The painting is 122 centimeters tall by 82 centimeters wide. This equates to 48 X 32.25 inches. The Virgin Mary is portrayed with young Jesus. Sometimes she is called a Hodegetria. In Polish that means, someone that leads or shows the way. Jesus appears to be giving a blessing while he holds a bible or book of gospels. It is thought the painting was created between the sixth and ninth century but was brought to the Czestochowa Monastery sometime in the fourteenth century.

According to information at the Monastery, Pope Clement XI performed a Canonical Coronation on September 8, 1717. Presidents, Heads of State and very important people along with thousands of tourists come each year to view this holy painting that is said to possess high holy powers.

This shrine is easily the most religious and popular one in Poland. Catholics from all over Poland make pilgrimages to the shrine every year. This nine day, one hundred forty mile event begins each August 6th and has been continuous since 1711. It continued throughout wars, even while being occupied by Germany in World War II.

Numerous legends and traditions are attributed to the Black Madonna. A tourist could easily spend several hours at the Monastery reading and learning about this lovely painting and what it means not only to Catholics but all citizens of Poland. It is a fact however, that historians have been researching the Black Madonna for centuries.

Our group moved next to the Wieliczka Salt Mine. When we learned we would tour a salt mine I thought, "HO HUM".

I could not have been more mistaken! It is safe to say this is one of the most unique tourist attractions we have ever visited. This Salt Mine is visited each year by over two million tourists that include Heads of State, Presidents, and a considerable number of Royalty.

Our guide provided a considerable amount of information about the mine as we moved from the Black Madonna to Wieliczka. I won't bore you with pages of statistics but there are a few things you should know.

Salt in the middle ages was used for preservation of meat and fish and was a valuable commodity. It was also a form of currency used by kings to finance their kingdoms' operations. Rock salt crystals were first found in this area in the late thirteenth century. Mining operations were begun here shortly after the discovery with the first shaft being sunk in the very late 13th century.

The mine consists of nine different levels. It is so large that tourists can only see about two percent. The first known tourist toured the mine in 1493. They have been keeping logs of tourists since the 1700s and those logs are considered valuable for research purposes. After signing the logs ourselves we were to begin our tour.

Every person to enter the mine must be a part of a group led by a guide employed by the mine. Groups are limited to twenty persons each.

Our group was assembled together for a short orientation by the guide. He outlined our journey. We will be taking the tourist route. The temperature was to be about sixty degrees. We would walk 3.5 kilometers which is 2.2 miles. There are 800 steps and we begin with 384 at the very start. The total descent is 135 meters which is 443 feet. We were told we would be taken out of the mine on a very small elevator at the end of the tour. We will be on the tour approximately two hours. Some in our group were concerned about claustrophobia. He advised paths were generally wide with high ceilings and there are numerous openings into large cavernous chambers. There are underground lakes, one of which people can purchase tickets for a boat ride. Claustrophobia did not turn out to be a problem with anyone.

We were told it would be best to use bathrooms prior to the tour because there are only two below and they could be very far apart.

There are over two thousand chambers in the mine. Many are elaborate and are as large as some of our largest basketball arenas. Some even contain salt chandeliers! Our route contains a goodly number. Many are quite elegant. No two chambers are alike. All are different.

St. King's Chapel and St. Anthony's Chapel are beautiful religious chambers and are used for religious ceremonies such as weddings, baptisms and regular church services. The Michalowice Chamber is one of the largest, very ornate and in the past received visitors with real orchestras playing chamber music. Our tour did not have the music today. It was quite the sight to see in person the underground saline lakes and chambers.

The elevator taking us out was very small and they packed every person they could on it. Mary and I waited to be the last on so she would not be crushed together in the back because she is slightly claustrophobic.

The mine has operated for over seven hundred years. It grew to nine levels, twenty six shafts and a depth of over a thousand feet. In 1996 production was halted and they no longer produce salt. However the mine still employs several hundred people dedicated to the conservation and enrichment of the chambers and benefit for the worldwide tourist community.

After our experience it was clear the importance of this tour. I cannot imagine coming to Poland without making this a must see destination.

We arrived to our hotel in Krakow in time for dinner and a night's rest. The next day is to be a big day. We are to visit Auschwitz in the afternoon!

Every morning on this tour we have been provided with outstanding American style breakfast buffets. This morning was no exception. Just saying!

Today's tour of Krakow focused on the Rynek Glowney Central Square, the Former Jewish District and the beauty of St. Mary's Basilica. We did enjoy these wonderful and emotional visits but I believe everyone was anxiously anticipating the afternoon visit to Auschwitz.

## AUSCHWITZ!

I am going to give you a brief bit of information regarding Auschwitz-Birkenau and the atrocities carried out by the Hitler regime between 1940 and its liberation in 1945. My main focus, however, will be on what Mary and I saw in person as we walked the paths where somewhere between one and one and a half million people were murdered.

Everyone would do themselves a favor to research Auschwitz-Birkenau because there is no way to fully describe or include the history of this concentration/death camp within this chapter. You will find it a sobering experience to research, but it does not compare to the gut gripping feeling you experience when you actually visit in person.

Auschwitz is not far from the town of Oswiecim, in Southern Poland. It is also not far from Krakow. Our guide said it was selected because it was close to many rail lines and centrally located within occupied parts of Europe by the Germans.

Our motor coach dropped us off quite a distance from the entrance. We walked along side railroad tracks and actual rail cars that had transported prisoners to their fate at Auschwitz. When we arrived at the main gate where we met our Auschwitz guide we stood below the iron archway that read, "Arbeit Macht Frei". It means in English, "Work Makes You Free."

The guide said upon arrival prisoners were separated by their ability to work. If you were able to work you were forced into hard labor making items that would aid the Germans in their war efforts. If you were not able to work, and that included all ages from the youngest children to pregnant women and the oldest of the group, you were at once ordered to, "take a shower".

They were herded into chambers that appeared to be bathhouses. Actually they were gas chambers made to look like a bathhouse. They were exposed to a poison gas. The guide said those not able to work were never processed or recorded so it was not possible to know the exact number executed here.

We were told that most of the people died in the gas chambers at Birkenau which was only a short distance from Auschwitz. Many people died from the hard labor, illness and malnutrition. There was an exhibit with pictures of people that died at the Auschwitz-Birkenau camps. It was a chilling moment when I found the picture of a child that had my exact birth date!

Mary is an identical twin and we toured a medical facility where terrible experiments were done on twins and young children. It was quite emotional for her, as well as everyone in our group.

We walked through buildings with exhibits behind glass windows. Each different exhibit would contain either piles of clothes, eyeglasses, suitcases, pairs of shoes, and the most chilling one was, several tons of human hair.

The dormitories were built to serve only a few thousand prisoners but they crowded four or five times the capacity into them. People had to sleep in shifts when they could find space to lie down.

Next we walked through the exact gas chambers I discussed earlier. It was almost as if you could feel the souls of those that had perished here. People spoke in hushed and muted tones. It was one of the saddest places in the world.

It was a very quiet ride from Auschwitz to our hotel in Krakow. The evening meal was also quiet and most of us retired early after a very emotional day.

We are to leave directly after an early breakfast for Prague. According to our guide this will be a fairly long drive from Krakow to Prague. Midday we were to stop at a castle for a tour but it turned out to be closed for renovation so we moved on to our Prague hotel after a short lunch break. The evening was on our own.

A very good city tour was provided the next morning. Prague has many memorials dedicated to the Jewish population that perished during World War II. One stood out in particular. A monument was erected at the point where hundreds of thousands of Jews boarded the fateful trains to Auschwitz.

Entire families, complete with young children, brought all the belongings they could carry with the promise they were being relocated to a much better place in life. Instead, they were shipped to Auschwitz to suffer the terrible atrocities of the Hitler regime we have described earlier.

The Charles Bridge is a major attraction in Prague. This bridge was started in 1357 by Charles IV and took forty five years to complete. It is made of sandstone blocks with towers on each side of the Vitava River. Over a period from 1683 to 1928 our guide advised thirty statues were installed on the bridge. Our guide claimed St. John of Nepomuk is the most famous. I took her word for it.

Poland is not a destination most people put high on their list of destinations in Europe. We found it to be an excellent vacation and we highly recommend it. It can be a very emotional but rewarding trip. There are numerous must see attractions in Poland. We are much better informed since we have visited these attractions and historic sites.

We flew directly back to Chicago the next morning.

# Egypt

The day is January 25, 2011. Mary and I are resting on a cruise ship in the Caribbean because we are anticipating hosting forty guests to Egypt for a twelve day visit that includes a seven day Nile River cruise in just two weeks. The documents are in our office and we've arranged a document pickup party when we return.

We figure we need this rest because hosting forty people through Egypt will be an exhausting couple weeks. It should be noted that we look for any excuse to justify lounging around on a cruise ship!

It is after dinner and we're in our cabin getting ready for bed. All at once I hear Mary scream, "Dick, Egypt is in terrible turmoil!" The TV was on and the news was covering 50,000 protesters in Tahrir Square in Cairo. They were protesting many things but the focus was to overthrow Egyptian President Hosni Mubarak. Over a period of several days, almost 900 were killed, over 6000 were injured and 90 police stations were burned.

This presented our office quite a problem. Of course airline tickets, tour operators and the cruise line had been paid in full. A very large amount of money was at stake for our clients. We worked long hours but are happy to say none of our clients lost any money because of the canceled trip. Our agency did suffer a large financial loss however!

Many years passed and we continued to have clients ask when we would be hosting a trip to Egypt? Our answer was always, "When we feel it is safe to travel in Egypt we will go there."

Seven years later a smaller but excited group departed for Cairo. This was almost the exact itinerary we wanted to do those many years before.

We departed Chicago on March 12 on an evening flight to Frankfurt, Germany where we had a very short connection for the flight to Cairo. There was an extremely long walk between our gates in Frankfurt and we also had to stand in very long lines at the passport control area. We made the flight to Cairo without much time to spare.

We were surprised to meet our tour director, Tarek Mustafa, before we had reached the passport control area. He collected all our passports and the money for the visa and he bypassed a long line of passengers applying for the Egypt visa. He came back a few minutes later with all our visas. Then we quickly were cleared through the passport control area and taken to our waiting motor coach. He made it so easy and fast to complete the entry process it was difficult to believe.

Upon arrival at the Cairo Marriott Hotel we were ushered into a private reception area with complimentary drinks while we completed the check-in. When check-in was completed, our guide, Tarek, presented a detailed briefing for protocol to follow while we're here in Egypt. We were given a meeting time for the morning tour. The rest of the day we were on our own.

We asked the concierge if it was safe for Americans to walk in the area around the hotel. He said yes but not to be out by ourselves after darkness. Several of us decided to walk in the area so we would stay awake for dinner at the hotel. Then it would be early to bed so we'd be ready for a full day tomorrow.

One of the most popular sites in Cairo is the Citadel. This is a large medieval fortress constructed high on a hill to protect from invasion. For over 700 years it was the home to Egyptian rulers and where the business of the government was conducted.

After the Citadel we moved on to the Mosque of Muhammad Ali, also known as the Alabaster Mosque. We visit here because it is probably the largest and most visited Mosque in Egypt. Besides its size, the Alabaster panels on the walls are beautiful to behold. It has very large minarets, over 270 feet, above ground. Everyone should take the time and physical effort to climb to the top of the minarets because you will have the finest view of Cairo possible.

Onward to our last stop prior to dinner. The Egyptian Museum was very interesting because it holds so many ancient artifacts. The exhibit of the young King Tutankhamun, known as King Tut, was very interesting. It was filled with fabulous artifacts recovered from his tomb. From what we read the tomb contained literally thousands of artifacts. The tomb was discovered in 1922 by an Egyptologist named Howard Carter. It is said that it took him and his crew over ten years to properly catalog everything that was in the tomb.

We return to the hotel in time to freshen up before we have a welcome drink and dinner. We will attend the sound and light show at the pyramids where we have reserved seats after dinner.

The light and sound show is very much worth seeing. It opens by lighting the Great Sphinx. The Sphinx narrates the history of the pyramids and those that built them. This was truly a fun and informative evening. If you make it to Cairo, don't miss this show.

Morning comes early for our group. Today we fly to Luxor where we visit the temple complex of Karnak before we board our cruise ship. One of our group is having a lot of trouble with all the walking that has been required. Mary and I had to figure a way for him to see everything and not be too tired or for that matter left off tours or having to stay on a bus while the rest of us enjoy the trip.

Karnak has had several names. Temple of Amun, Throne of the Two Lands, and Selected Spot are a few of them. Karnak is the largest religious building in the world according to our guide, Tarek. Ancient Egyptians 2000 BC believed this is where the world was created and they built this massive complex to honor the God Amun on this spot. Many believe it was also an observatory. It is still possible to see artwork where these ancient drawings still have the original colors. We will return here later in the cruise for another sound and light show.

We leave Karnak and travel to embark our ship, the MS *Medea*. The MS *Medea* is one of the most luxurious Nile River Cruise Ships. It is rated, and from our experience, certainly qualifies for its five star rating.

Mary and I met with Tarek about the problem with our client having trouble walking. He suggested the three of us discuss this with the cruise director. We checked with the Purser and the ship did have a wheelchair we could use. We thought a wheelchair could be a partial answer but the ground we usually had been walking over was rough and very rocky. Pushing him in a wheelchair would be very difficult for anyone in our group. After a lengthy discussion we suggested that we pay one of the ship's crew to go on the tours with us and push our friend in the wheelchair.

The cruise director had to get approval from the Captain to do this. It was approved and the young man assigned to us was very young and very strong. I'm certain he was happy to pick up the extra money we would pay him for his help. This arrangement worked out very well. We were all relieved that our friend would be able to enjoy everything everyone else would see.

We dock March 16th at the Dendera complex. This area contains two temples. The Temple of Hathor and the Temple of Dendera. Temple of Hathor is one of the best preserved temples in Egypt. Hathor was a significant Goddess. She was said to promote the virtues of motherhood and feminine love. When you see these temples and the size of them and the stone columns it is difficult to imagine how they had the ability to construct these marvelous temples over three thousand years before Christ! These temples were built to honor her.

Meals aboard the MS *Medea* were excellent. We were surprised that we had nightly entertainment. Sometimes locals were brought on board to perform typical Egyptian ancient dance and entertainment. Other times we had a piano player and a singer. One evening everyone dressed in Egyptian costumes. It was a lot of fun to see everyone dressed as Egyptians!

**Dick and Mary in Egypt**

After Dendera we sailed the Nile to the Temple of Horus. This temple was one of the largest and youngest of temples. It was built beginning in 57 AD and continued to be constructed for the next 180 years. Horus was worshiped with the head and sometimes the body of a falcon as the ruler of the skies. This temple does contain a description of Cleopatra and her son Caesarian, whose father was Julius Caesar.

After our visit to The Temple Horus and the smaller Temple of Kom Ombo, we sailed on to Aswan. Here we visit the Aswan High Dam. We travel by motorboat to the Temple of Isis. It was built 690 years BC to honor the Goddess of Isis and remained viable for almost a thousand years. It is well preserved on this unusual island location.

March 19th we take the optional excursion and take a forty five minute flight from Aswan to AbuSimbel. We are taken to the Temple of Ramses II which is walking distance to Nefertari's Temple of Hathor. We tour the interior of both temples. The carvings and art inside are well preserved. Both temples were threatened in 1960 by a proposal to raise Lake Nasser but UNESCO led a fight to save them and thankfully they prevailed. This was a full day excursion and very much worth the time.

Close to Aswan were several quaint Nubian Villages. We did visit one. It was full of very good small restaurants for lunch. These Nubian Villages surprise us because they are painted in bright colors and are quite beautiful to see.

The 21st of March was a delightful full day of sailing the Nile. We spent the day on the top deck having some cocktails and viewing the scenery. Tonight we're back to Luxor where we will take in the sound and light show.

Some of our friends thought it would be a repeat of the show we saw in Cairo. Not so. There were similarities in spots but the setting was considerably different. Walking to the show area between the pillars on the rough paths was difficult and not very safe in the dark. Mary and I had provided each of our clients a small flashlight before we left home and told everyone to be sure to pack them. It was very helpful to have them. Of course some did not bring them but we had packed some extras so all was good.

It was a long walk to the bleachers but the setting was in front of a beautiful lake area. It was a good show and a good night. Everyone enjoyed the evening a great deal.

Today we disembark the MS *Medea*. We have our luggage out early, have breakfast and board buses for the Valley of Kings before we fly back to Cairo.

For over five hundred years powerful Egyptians and Pharaohs were entombed in the Valley of the Kings. Tombs range from one small chamber to one hundred twenty chambers. They date back to sixteen centuries before Christ. There is constant exploration in this area by Archaeologists. New tombs have been located in 2005 and two in 2008.

The most famous discovery was the tomb of King Tutankhamun by Howard Carter in 1923. We were able to enter this famous tomb. It is said there is a curse of the Pharaohs on those that enter. We risked it anyway!

We had a good amount of time in the Valley and did visit a couple more tombs before boarding our bus to the airport and our return flight to Cairo. Our home for the next two nights will again be the Cairo Marriott.

Tarek has us up early for breakfast and an early departure for the Pyramids. We are there before the throng of tourists and are able to actually go inside one of the Pyramids. That was only possible because we arrived early. "Early is good!" says Dick.

The Great Pyramid of Giza is the oldest and largest Pyramid in Giza. It was built approximately two thousand six hundred years before Christ with stones from as far away as Aswan. It is one of the seven manmade wonders of the world still in good shape.

We leave here for a visit to the Great Sphinx and a group photo before we enjoy our camel ride!

***Picture Perfect Travel Group***

It is just a short bus ride to the camel staging area. Mary and I were interested because from this area we could see a road race being held on the highway. It turns out we are in Cairo on the day of the Cairo Marathon.

That would have been a tough race because it was in the desert and the temperature had to be close to ninety five or one hundred degrees! We were content to ride our camels!

The camel ride was a real highlight of the trip. There is a very specific way to saddle up and mount the camel. There were a lot of laughs on this hour long ride. We got some very funny and interesting pictures before we boarded our coach to return to the hotel. Tonight is our farewell dinner and cocktail party.

We had an issue with the hotel for seating the group that evening. I went to handle the problem with the head waiter. It was taken care of easily. The dining area outside in the hotel gardens was surrounded on all sides by very tall walls. The hotel had very obvious high security everywhere.

As I was talking to the head waiter I heard gunshots outside the walls. He told me that was a very common thing in Cairo and obviously did not want to talk about it. He assured me we are safe within the walls of their garden and not to worry.

I talked to Tarek about this. He said that was true but he told me something none of us had thought about. On every motor coach and tour there were always two friends of our guide and driver that joined us. They didn't seem too interested in mixing with our group but they were friendly. Tarek told me they were armed guards that had been with our group for the entire trip!

Egypt needed and wanted the American Tourist. They did not want to have an international incident. Never did we feel threatened at any time. I waited until we were home before I told the group about what I had learned that last night.

We hardly got our sheets warm in the hotel that night. Our transfer to the airport was at 2:30 A.M. We flew home again through Frankfurt, Germany. It was a very long time before we made it home for a good night's sleep but this trip was well worth the long travel hours.

Egypt was one of our very favorite trips and fulfilled one of my childhood dreams of seeing the Pyramids and Temples.

# Osaka, Japan

Mary is the incoming President of the Rotary Club in Rock Island, Illinois. The incoming President is always requested to represent the club at the International Convention of Rotary. Most incoming Presidents attend their Conventions. The club pays for the airline ticket, the hotel, and food expenses.

Her Convention is in Osaka, Japan and she is enthusiastic to represent her Rotary Club. When she explores the hotel costs for convention hotels she finds they are far too expensive. She finds a Comfort Inn within walking distance of the hotels where we can catch transportation to the convention center. Her price was considerably less than the convention hotels and she felt really good about saving the club so much money.

She very nicely invited me to accompany her. My cost was only my airline ticket and food expenses. I should point out here that the following year I was the incoming President of Kiwanis and she accompanied me to my International Convention in Honolulu, Hawaii! Quid Pro Quo!

We flew Japan Air from Chicago non-stop to Osaka, Japan. I've been a pilot for many years and not much about airplanes scare me. On final approach to the Osaka Airport it was raining and lightning so hard it was impossible to see. The plane was crabbed into a forty-five-degree angle to the runway by the wind and that would make for a difficult and bumpy landing. As we broke through the ceiling we found the runway, corrected the crab and greased the landing! These pilots were darn good.

Immigration and customs were very easy and we found a customer service kiosk to ask for help getting to our hotel. Mary presented the hotel name and address to the customer service representative. He said he knew the hotel and would write directions on a card so we could present it to a taxi driver when we arrived downtown. The card was written in those unreadable characters. He also helped us get some Japanese Currency from the ATM.

It was almost an hour train ride from the airport to the train station downtown. We got front row seats looking directly ahead and even through the rain it was a fun train ride.

Just prior to entering the train station we went below ground level. Departing the train it became immediately clear language is going to be a really big issue. We took the escalator to ground level to find the taxi stand.

When it was our turn the taxi driver put our luggage in the trunk. We handed him the card with the funny little characters on it. He smiled and took off driving with Mary and me in the seat behind him. After maybe fifteen minutes driving, he pulled to the curb, parked and turned around to me and shrugged his shoulders. I smiled and shrugged my shoulders back at him.

He pulled out a phone and called someone. He looked at me again smiled and took off driving again. A few minutes later, we pull up in front of a very nice looking building and we're relieved to be here. He got out and I started to get out also and he held up one finger as if asking me to stay. I followed him into the building anyway. Turns out, we're at a police station! Okay, I'm willing to wait in the car.

He returned, we drive again and make a couple turns and behold we are at the front door of our hotel. Before we let him go we confirmed with the desk that we were indeed at the correct hotel just to be certain. We did this because once in Ft. Lauderdale about midnight a taxi driver dropped us at the wrong hotel. We confirmed we were in the correct hotel and very glad to be there.

This hotel was in what they called the old town area. It was very clean but the room we had was the smallest room ever. There was only a small area to walk at the end of the bed and one side of the bed was against the wall. The other side had about eighteen inches to the other wall. It did contain a small bathroom. Like I said, Mary got a really good rate that saved her Rotary Club a lot of money. It did include a very good breakfast buffet each morning and it turned out almost everyone there was registered at the Rotary Convention.

Arriving a couple days early gave us some time to rest and also time to visit a few tourist sites. The front desk assured us we were only a couple blocks from a commuter line that would take us to the Imperial Palace in Kyoto. Yes, they told us it was easy and we wouldn't have any problems. Anytime someone tells us that, we know we're in deep trouble.

It was easy to find the entrance to the underground rail system. We had to purchase tickets to Kyoto but there was no attendant, just automated ticket machines. Mary and I were just standing there puzzled because it was all in Japanese and we didn't have a clue.

A very well dressed Japanese gentleman approached us. For certain he knew we were in trouble. He spoke very good English and he helped us purchase the round trip tickets. He also told us which train to take, which stop to get off for Kyoto and also the one to get off when we returned. We thanked him over and over but he said he was just glad to help.

Kyoto is beautiful and we walked around the ancient Imperial Palace and its gardens. This was a very impressive Palace and gardens. I took many very beautiful pictures. Without the help of the gentleman to purchase tickets we would have missed a really nice day trip.

One thing we had not seen before was the way restaurants would display their menu items in the window. In the United States we take pictures, show pricing with a description of the meal. In Japan they would prepare a meal and then cover the entire meal with a clear plastic polyurethane much like you would finish a wooden table or even a floor. They display these in the window with a price. I guess enclosed in polyurethane these meals will last a very long time because no air can reach the meal.

Not far from our hotel was a very good British fish and chips restaurant. On nights when we did not have convention activities we enjoyed the fish and chips.

The Rotary Convention was one of the largest conventions they ever had. They estimated forty thousand participants with a very high percent being the Japanese. We stood in a huge crowd outside the convention center waiting for the doors to open. The Japanese people are very lovely people but they are not very tall. As we stand in the crowd we watched over the heads of thousands of people and of course Mary and I were the tallest people in sight, at least head and shoulders above them!

One thing we remember about the convention food was a cheeseburger we had from a McDonald's. It was by far the best double cheeseburger we've ever had from a McDonald's. They were far superior to anything we have in McDonald's in the States. Hot, juicy, and lots of melted cheese.

This was an outstanding convention. International Conventions, whether they are Rotary, Kiwanis or other service clubs, educate the members about current local and international programs. That information when brought back to local service clubs provides new revenue streams and beneficial programs for needy organizations. Mary and I are both honored to have served in leadership positions with National Service Organizations.

We left time after the convention for a very moving visit to Hiroshima. This trip would be an early morning trip on the bullet train from Osaka to Hiroshima. We would have several hours at the memorial before returning to Osaka again on the bullet train.

The bullet train between Osaka and Hiroshima takes only one hour and twenty five minutes. It is two hundred twenty four miles between cities. The Conductor seemed to take a liking to us. He would come by our seats and say, "In thirty seconds you will see a palace." We could see our speed on an indicator above the door between cars and it stayed steady at 300 kilometers per hour. Being a runner I knew that was 186 miles per hour. When we passed the Palace at 186 miles per hour it was nothing more than a blur. We were gracious and thanked him for taking care of us.

Hiroshima was a very important military city. It was headquarters for several Japanese units and a very important port for shipping military supplies. That made it an obvious target. On August 6, 1945, the United States dropped "Little Boy" on the city of Hiroshima. The first nuclear bomb in history was dropped this date at 8:15 A.M. It destroyed over 70 percent of the city and over the course of time over one hundred fifty thousand men, women and children lost their lives. A very small percent were military personnel.

The day we were in Hiroshima there were dozens of school groups. We were told a trip to Hiroshima is mandatory for every student in Japan prior to graduating from high school. We listened to school choirs singing at the Peace Memorial. We read every plaque and viewed each part of the area at the Peace Memorial. What happened here was a necessary act of war. We were told that even with the loss of lives here, many more would have lost their lives on both sides of the war if they had not dropped the bomb.

We rode the bullet train back to Osaka that evening in a quiet and sober mood. You absolutely cannot visit Hiroshima without feeling a sadness that almost overwhelms you because you know many innocent people lost their lives on August 6, 1945.

Our flight left Osaka at 4:30 P.M. for Los Angeles. We arrived Los Angeles at 10:35 A.M. which was the same day. How strange was that? We cleared immigration in LAX and flew back to Chicago.

Mary took a lot of good information back to her Rotary Club but we also learned a great deal about history and how it affects all our lives today.

# Burgundy & Provence

In April, Mary and I had the privilege of having the President of Uniworld Boutique River Cruises, Mr. Guy Young, join us at our table at the Mast Vacation Partners Conference where I was the current Chairman and CEO. It was my distinct pleasure to introduce him as one of our featured speakers.

During our dinner conversation we discussed a new cruise ship that he and the company were very excited about. The SS. *Catherine* was their newest and most elegant ship in their fleet. It was also sailing an itinerary we had not sailed before from Lyon to Avignon, France.

We decided this would be a good trip for us. It was selling so well we could not get reservations until November. Two couples that were friends of ours liked what we were telling them about the ship and the itinerary and decided to join us.

The cruise line air department provided the best flight schedule for a reasonable price. They also coordinated all six of us on the same flights.

Our flight itinerary called for us to leave our International Airport in Moline, Illinois on the direct flight to Detroit and then to Amsterdam. We would clear immigration into the European Union in Amsterdam and then take an inter European flight to Lyon, France, arriving in Lyon at 11:05 A.M. local time. Upon arrival in Lyon the cruise line would transfer us to the SS. *Catherine*.

Three hours prior to arrival in Amsterdam there was a disturbance a few rows ahead of us. The flight attendant came to Mary and said one of our friends was having a medical emergency and asked if we could assist the crew. Our friend was having serious issues and we put her on the floor of the airplane by a bulkhead where there was more room and would not completely block the aisle.

A call was put out to see if a Doctor was on board. There was, and the Doctor and flight attendant tended to our friend. Mary was authorized to work with the First Class flight attendant to give information to the

Captain so he could arrange for an ambulance for her on arrival in Amsterdam. The airport in Amsterdam does have excellent hospital facilities on site.

I worked with other flight attendants to give information about our friend's luggage and have it secured for them. In all our flights throughout the world this was the one and only time I ever saw a landing made with a passenger lying flat on the floor.

An announcement was made for everyone to keep their seats until the EMTs could board the plane and take our friend off first. Mary and I offered to stay with them but the husband said there would be little we could do since she was in the care of medical professionals. He said we should continue with the others.

We continued on to Lyon and boarded the ship. As we checked in I advised the Purser's desk about our friend's situation.

As we were checking in, the Cruise Director came over and introduced herself. They have amazing memories. Our Cruise Director, Emmanuel Bonneau, recognized us and told us she had sailed with us previously on the SS. *River Princess*!

The next morning on our way to breakfast, we stopped by the Purser's desk to see what, if anything, could be done for our friends not being able to make the trip. To say we were surprised is an understatement! She said, "They arrived late last night and are in the dining room and are having breakfast!"

Apparently her illness was caused by something to do with air pressure differences during the flight. The Doctors in Amsterdam recognized the issue. They stabilized her, gave her medicine and released her to travel. The airline made special arrangements to get them to our cruise ship. It did help that we were not sailing until the next afternoon from Lyon.

To say the SS. *Catherine* was elegant is quite an understatement. Beautiful artwork adorned all the walls. The art onboard the ship was said to be worth millions. The chandeliers, the furniture and all accents were breath taking.

We were cruising through the most famous wine country in Europe. There were shore excursions in each port where we could taste great wines and at one stop we had lunch at a French Baron's house with excellent wine choices. Everyone was having a great trip. Great ship, good food, good wine and a staff that anticipated everybody's wants and needs.

Friday we had toured an area that Romans had occupied and developed two thousand years ago. Roman arches were quite impressive to visit. UNESCO has designated this as a historical preservation site.

Each night just before dinner we would meet to discuss the next day's activities. On Friday night our Cruise Director Emmanuel said we would be traveling through some thunderstorms during the night on our way to Avignon. We would be docked in Avignon until disembarking Sunday morning for our return flights home.

During the night lightning, thunder and rain rattled the entire night. The lightning and thunder made it almost impossible to sleep. This turned out to be a vicious storm. By breakfast time we had docked in Avignon. Another cruise line was docked directly behind us.

Cruise ships dock on a levy that keeps the river from flooding the town. Usually you would leave the ship and walk up steps to the top of the levy. The downtown area is directly on the other side of the levy.

When we went to breakfast the river was rising rapidly and had risen to the point where our ship's gangway was only a few feet from the top of the levy. During breakfast an announcement was made there would be a mandatory meeting for all passengers in the lounge at 10 A.M.

We were told we had one hour to pack all belongings and evacuate the ship. It was expected the river would rise above the levy and flood Avignon. Buses would be available to take everyone to a Five Star Marriott Hotel that was on high ground.

The crew was very helpful in getting everyone and their luggage to the coaches. When we arrived at the hotel, lunch was ready and we were told any shore excursions that were scheduled would operate as scheduled. Upon our return from the shore excursions Uniworld had set up an open bar along with an excellent dinner complete with chamber music.

It pays to book top-of-the-line companies when you travel. The cruise line docked behind our ship was kept on the ship until Sunday morning when they had to disembark for the airport. No open bar, no shore excursions, no five star hotel and no chamber music! We met some of those passengers at the airport and when they heard what Uniworld had done for us they were not too happy.

Water reached within a few inches of the top of the levy but it did not flow over the top or flood the city.

Our flights home were uneventful and we all felt we had a great vacation. When we returned I wrote Guy Young, President of Uniworld, a letter giving him names of outstanding crew members and asked him to personally pass along our gratitude for their very fine work.

# New Year's on Jewel of the Seas

We woke up on New Year's Day after having a very nice evening at a house party New Year's Eve at the home of one of our close friends. It was very nice and we had a good time. However, we had done that for the past couple years and we looked at each other and said, "We need to do something different next year."

The next day at our office I looked to see if a cruise would work out for the next year. I couldn't believe it! I found a seven day cruise December 29 through January 5 on Royal Caribbean's *Jewel of the Seas*. It sailed round trip from San Juan. It had a great itinerary with ports of call in Barbados, Grenada, Dominica, St. Martin and St. Thomas.

Pricing was so reasonable I questioned if it might be a mistake. I booked Mary and me in a nice balcony cabin. Mary's sister also booked a balcony cabin and we were set for the next New Years.

We told a couple friends what we were doing. They told their friends and it was only a couple days until we had clients actually standing in line in our office to join us. I turned these reservations into a group booking and we had over sixty people booked to cruise with us.

Cruise ships are decorated so beautifully for the Christmas and New Year's sailings. Our group was very happy and things were going well. I really believe the best way to celebrate a new year is on a cruise ship or on a midnight run. This year was the cruise ship. We boarded the ship on December 29th.

After a day at sea we docked on December 31st in Barbados. When we returned to the ship after our city tour, Mary and I were informed that one of the ladies in our group had fallen while leaving a restaurant and had seriously broken her ankle. She was in a hospital in Barbados undergoing surgery as the ship sailed. We were all sad for her and her husband because of the injury and also because it had happened on New Year's Eve.

The New Year's celebration aboard the *Jewel of the Seas* was spectacular. Music, balloons, noise makers, free champagne and confetti made the evening one to remember always. The ship also included a midnight buffet with some of the best food you could imagine. Everyone said they had one of the best times they have ever had on a New Year's Eve!

*Dick & Mary, New Year's on the Jewel of the Seas*

New Year's Day we docked in Grenada. Just prior to sailing that afternoon, we were pleasantly surprised to find our friend with the broken ankle being pushed by her husband in a wheelchair and back on the ship.

As it turned out when she fell in Barbados a Royal Caribbean staff member came to her aid. He suggested they go to a private hospital rather than a government funded hospital. They were taken promptly to the operating room. Of course they required payment in advance many thousands of dollars. Fortunately they had credit cards that covered the bill. We had also sold them trip insurance so they were reimbursed for most of the cost after we helped them file a claim when they returned home.

We were told the Royal Caribbean staff in Barbados had worked above their call of duty to see that they were not only taken to a hospital to get prompt care but also to find a way for them to rejoin the ship.

The next day, Wednesday, we docked in Dominica. After returning from our island tour we had lunch with another lady we knew well. She said she and her husband had enjoyed the New Year's party and this cruise more than any other New Year's she could remember. She thanked us for organizing such a great trip. It is sad to note a few days after the cruise, she passed away.

When we have large groups on a ship, Mary and I usually try to provide a cocktail party a day or two prior to the cruise ending. Our party usually includes complimentary drinks and snacks just prior to the dinner hour. This time we had hired a piano player that really rocked the party. Everyone had a marvelous time. For some reason my friends seem to have more fun when their drinks are on my bill! This cocktail party was the ideal way to finish the celebration of the start of a New Year.

On Friday we visited St. Thomas. This American possession is one of the favorite islands for tourists in the Caribbean. Many of our friends spent the day at Señor Frogs preparing themselves for the next day's flight home and the cold weather reported we have there.

All of the group met on the pier at the time I had designated. I had hired a motor coach to transfer the group to the airport. It was quite late arriving. Of course people in San Juan work at a different pace. The bus finally arrived and we drove the group to the airport.

# Lutherland

It is the year of the 500th Anniversary of the Protestant Reformation. Martin Luther is said to have nailed his list of 95 objections, to Catholic beliefs and practices to the door of his home church on October 31, 1517.

Taking such a stand with his "95 Theses" was a direct challenge to the Pope and Roman Authority. Martin Luther was a very well educated person. He was a University Lecturer, and an Augustinian Monk.

Our Pastor, Reverend DR. Willers, was interested in visiting the homeland of Martin Luther. Pastor wanted to learn more first hand about Martin Luther. He worked with Mary and me to formulate an itinerary that would visit places where Martin Luther lived, was educated, taught and passed away.

He approved an itinerary we put together and we offered it to the congregation. Several members decided to join Pastor and us.

On June 16th we motor coached the group to Chicago for our 4:45PM flight to Amsterdam where we would clear immigration and customs into the European Union. We then change planes arriving in Berlin at noon.

We met our guide, Cheryl, at baggage claim in Berlin. She is a history teacher at a University in Berlin but does tour guiding during her summer months. The first thing we do is a city tour of Berlin that includes a stop at the famed Checkpoint Charlie. Checkpoint Charlie was a major gateway between East and West Germany during the cold war. The original guardhouse is now on exhibit at the Allied Museum in Berlin.

There are some original pieces and markings of the Berlin wall at this Checkpoint Charlie location. When we were there, actors dressed in authentic uniforms were available to have pictures taken with the tourists. Of course there was a fee for the pictures. It is my understanding the Berlin City Government stopped this process recently because the actors were gouging the tourists with extremely high prices.

We leave early for Leipzig. It is a short drive, a little over an hour, and we arrive at St. Thomas Church. This church was originally a Catholic Church but during the reformation it became a Lutheran Church and is still used today as a Lutheran Church.

Johann Sebastian Bach was a music director at this church for twenty seven years, 1723 until he passed away in 1750. His remains are buried at this church. We were very fortunate to be treated to a magnificent Bach organ concert.

After lunch we moved on to Wittenberg. Wittenberg was very important to Martin Luther. There are many memorials here dedicated to Martin Luther and the Luther Memorial was named a UNESCO World Heritage Site in 1996. Because of Martin Luther's influence and work in this city it has become a top tourist site in Germany.

We were privileged to tour a part of the Augustinian monastery where Martin Luther lived as a Monk and later lived with his wife and children after he purchased it. Our second day in Wittenberg we had a walking tour where we saw the home where Martin Luther was born and also the home where he passed away. They called it his death house.

Next morning we moved on to Erfurt. We were pleased to see how medieval the city was. The Erfurt Cathedral sitting high on Cathedral Hill was an awe inspiring sight.

We did a walking tour that included the old Merchants Bridge, the Synagogue and Citadel. Finally we drove by the Erfurt University where Martin Luther was a student prior to entering the monastery.

Cheryl, our guide being a University history teacher, was extremely well educated about Martin Luther. I kept copious notes of the history and statistics. She was a fountain of knowledge and our Pastor, Reverend Dr. Willers was happy to be here in the land of Martin Luther learning so many things new to him about Martin Luther.

After Erfurt we moved on to Eisenach where we visit the Wartburg Castle. This castle has had many famous residents but the reason for our visit was to see the place where Cheryl told us Martin Luther spent almost a year here for his own safety. He stayed here under an assumed name of Junker Jorg (Knight George) after he had been excommunicated by Pope Leo X because of the 95 Theses. While here Martin Luther translated the New Testament from Greek to German. She said it took him only ten weeks to make the translation. Cheryl offered however that some locals believe he did also work on the translation in Coburg. We will be in Coburg tomorrow.

The Wartburg Castle is impressive because it is built on a high cliff above the city of Eisenach. This tour has taken us to many locations where the castles are set high on bluffs. Germany is literally filled with castles on high sites. Each one is good for the photographers in our group.

Coburg & Rothenburg were well preserved cities and did not sustain much damage from the war. Rothenburg is the gateway to the Black Forest.

We over night in Rothenburg and Cheryl has arranged the Night Watchman Tour for our group. I highly recommend this tour. You get a walking tour of the city by a very knowledgeable guide that gives you city history with a great deal of good humor.

The long drive to Oberammergau through the Black Forest was beautiful. We arrived in Oberammergau, the home of the Passion Play that is held every ten years, early afternoon.

Our hotel, The Alte Post was right in the center of the downtown. According to their literature, the hotel is family run and dates back to 1612. The rooms were small but clean and quaint. We enjoyed this hotel a great deal. Our room had a good view of the downtown but the view of the Alps was absolutely stunning. The women in the group loved the fact there was great shopping and dining just a few feet outside the front door of the hotel.

We wanted to see Oberammergau even though the Passion Play was not to be held for three more years. The theater venue was only a few blocks away. It was a pleasant evening and many shops were open so we enjoyed our free time looking for things for kids and grandkids.

Today we visit some very important tourist sites. We travel to Hohenschwangau to visit Neuschwanstein Castle. In short we visit the city where King Ludwig's Castle was built.

Ludwig's father King Ludwig I died unexpectedly and Ludwig II became King at age eighteen. According to Cheryl he was not ready to be King and things did not go well for him. He ultimately was declared insane and removed from the throne. Shortly thereafter he committed suicide.

King Ludwig's Castle is beautifully perched high above the city. It is reported to be the most photographed castle in Europe. Our group certainly took plenty of pictures. We were able to view it from the outside but we had not purchased tickets in advance so we did not see the inside.

After leaving Ludwig's Castle we stopped at the Eagle's Nest. This restaurant was built on a very high rocky mountain top. Hitler was recorded as being here several times but did not like it because of the height. We entered a tunnel and walked quite a distance before we found an elevator. The elevator didn't look too safe but we rode to the top in it and back down. Cheryl had not given us much time so we looked around and took many pictures and returned to our motor coach.

We over night tonight in Salzburg. First thing after breakfast we take a city tour that includes a walking tour and a visit to Mozart's home. Many took the cable car to the top where the fortress s located. We had been to Salzburg before and we went to a restaurant we knew from before. This restaurant is close to the entrance of the cable car. It was very very small but we remembered that it serves the largest bratwurst and kraut we've ever enjoyed.

Reunion with our bratwurst was a wonderful occasion! They were just as good on our return as they were the first time. I don't remember the name of the restaurant but it is the only restaurant in that area. Face the cable car entrance and look directly to your right. It's only a few feet from you and well worth the visit.

We drive then to Munich in time for dinner in one of their numerous beer gardens. We are here for two nights prior to returning home.

This last day will be an emotional day. We do a city tour for a couple hours before leaving the city for a visit to Dachau, a Nazi concentration camp not far from Munich.

Dachau was built originally to hold political enemies of Hitler. Cheryl told stories of cruel behavior against prisoners. Many were forced to work until they died of malnutrition and exhaustion. Brutal treatment such as floggings, tree hanging and standing at attention for extremely long hours. The prison inmates soon included Jews, German and Austrian criminals as well as anyone that happened to be an enemy of Hitler.

What went on at Dachau was terrible with so many thousands of people murdered. Mary and I had also visited Auschwitz and seeing yet another Nazi concentration camp further demonstrated the terrible depths of treatment Hitler subjected on those incarcerated in these camps. The memories of these camps will live with us forever.

We returned to Munich just in time to be taken to the restaurant for our farewell dinner. This was a really good evening. The food was excellent and they had a polka band that was really good. In fact Mary and I dazzled everyone with our polka dancing!

Cheryl had asked us to remain seated when the show was over so she could make an announcement. The announcement was that she had sent the bus driver to his home and the group had to walk about a mile or mile and a half to the hotel!

To say we were shocked does not begin to cover how we felt. In the hundreds of trips we've hosted around the world, never have we been stranded with no way back to the hotel.

Two things were wrong about this. First, we had people that could never walk that far, and second, the directions to the hotel were not clear. Mary and I sent those not able to walk to the hotel back in a taxi. The rest of the group decided to walk with us.

We thought Cheryl would walk with us but she wanted to stop at a bar in a shopping center close by. We were on our own and of course got lost. Long ago we learned to take a business card from the hotel with us and with the help of friendly policemen our group made it back.

Cheryl had been a very knowledgeable guide. She provided a wealth of information along the way. Our people wanted to know about her gratuity. My message to them was to let their heart be their guide. The lack of transportation to the hotel greatly affected how people felt about her overall performance. Many were worried about our morning transfer to the airport.

Fortunately our early morning transfer to the airport was on time. The driver and our bus was different. We left the hotel at 5:00AM. Our flight from Munich to Amsterdam was at 9:25 AM, arriving at 11:00 AM. We had a short connection of only an hour and twenty five minutes. The flight left Amsterdam at 12:25 PM and we arrived in Chicago 1:55 PM Chicago time.

This trip was somewhat different from the usual groups we host because the most of the emphasis was educational. We liked it for many reasons. It was educational but it had beautiful scenery, marvelous photo opportunities and was actually a great amount of fun.

# Scandinavia & Russia

It's August 9th and our group of eleven people is seated at the Moline International Airport waiting to board our 5 P.M. flight to Detroit. We then connect to our overnight flight to London. When we arrive in London we are to be met by our limo driver and then taken to the Port of Harwich, England where we will embark the beautiful Royal Caribbean cruise ship, the *Jewel of the Seas,* for a twelve day cruise through Scandinavia which features an overnight stay in St. Petersburg, Russia.

We're happy when the announcement is made, "We will be boarding your flight in ten minutes." Not so happy five minutes later when they announce, "Your flight is canceled."

Mary and I sprint to the gate agent to see what can be done to get us to London on time. We were first in line but we had to re-book eleven people.

We were told there was no way to get us to London on Delta in time to make our cruise! Mary and I explained that eleven people will miss a cruise if they cannot find a way to get us there the next day before noon.

The gate agent searched and found a United flight leaving Moline in just a few minutes for Chicago that would connect to a flight from Chicago direct to London. It would get us there in time if we could get all of us re-booked, get our luggage off the Delta flight and re-checked on the United flight, and physically get everybody to the United gate before it leaves the gate.

A second Delta agent came to our gate and assisted in our re-book and luggage transfer. Mary and I sprinted from the Delta gate to the United gate and did our best to keep the United flight from leaving without our entire group. Airlines do not like to leave an airport even a minute late if they can help it and those United people were not happy with us!

Our group was doing their best to get from Delta to United but it was quite a long walk. Our pleading along with the fact we could show the United people the last person was within sight worked out and we all made the flight to Chicago.

When we arrived in Chicago I called our limo company and advised them we were arriving London on United in place of Delta at a different time. They assured me that was no problem. The London office would be notified and we would be picked up without a problem.

Our biggest concern was whether we would see our luggage when we arrived in London. How pleased and surprised we were when we went to baggage claim and found every piece of luggage had arrived without any problem. Things are going well.

The instructions from the limo company told us to collect our luggage, clear immigration and customs then proceed into the general population of the airport. We would be met by someone holding a sign with our name on it.

We did as instructed but no one was there to meet us. I left the group and went to the Delta terminal to see if they were there. Nobody here either. I went to the airport customer service and had the company paged.

No answer. I had their local office number and called it. They assured me their man was there. We did everything we knew to find him but to no avail.

At this point we had spent considerable time to find the limo and we were running out of time. It was a several hour trip from the airport to the pier. I checked taxi cabs but nobody wanted to drive that far, plus it would have cost a fortune if they would do it.

If we miss the cruise today we would have to fly to Copenhagen to join the ship plus we'd miss two days of the cruise and have two extra hotel nights. Frustration was setting in when we found a young man that was handling the transfer services for Royal Caribbean. His name was Will. He was the nicest person and wanted to be very helpful to our group. When we returned home I sent a letter to Royal Caribbean management to tell them what a jewel he was getting our group to the *Jewel*!

He said he had only one bus left going to Harwich and he had just enough seats to handle our group. Rather than continue with the futile attempt to find our limo we joined the Royal Caribbean bus for the trip to

Harwich. We actually were the last people to board the ship before it sailed!

I remember when we boarded the ship we were warmly greeted and the check-in was one of the smoothest we ever experienced. All of our group felt as if we were treated like royalty the entire cruise. Maybe it was because we had such a stressful beginning but it certainly felt good.

With the next day at sea our group, especially Mary and me, took some much needed rest and relaxation. There was time to review our itinerary. We have six ports of call. Copenhagen, Denmark, Stockholm, Sweden. Helsinki, Finland, St. Petersburg, Russia, Tallinn, Estonia and Gothenburg, Sweden.

Having been to Copenhagen and Stockholm previously we got off the ship and enjoyed the areas for shopping on the waterfront. Some of the group enjoyed Tivoli Theme Park and Gardens which is one of the most popular tourist attractions in Copenhagen. Copenhagen is the capital of Denmark and complete with its suburbs has only about a million three hundred thousand population.

Stockholm, the capital of Sweden has close to two million citizens in the metro area. There is a lot to see and do here but the thing I remember best is being on the top deck as we made our way to dock in Stockholm. The scenery as you pass between the numerous islands is beautiful and unique to most ports of call. If you go to Stockholm be certain to know exactly when you will be arriving and go out on deck to see the views. Many people miss this experience. They definitely should not miss this approach to Stockholm!

Helsinki is another capital city. It's about the size of Copenhagen in population. We took a city tour that was quite interesting. We like the city tours off the ship. Usually you learn the history and see the most important parts of the city. I do believe however, we were looking ahead to tomorrow's stop in St. Petersburg.

There were a lot of options for sightseeing in St. Petersburg. We were to arrive early morning and overnight there and leave late evening the next day.

One interesting optional excursion was a flight to Moscow. We did consider that but decided against it for a couple reasons. If you book excursions that are offered by the cruise line you do not need a visa to enter Russia. However, if you want to go off on your own you will need to apply for an entry visa. At the time a visa cost was $350.00 per person. You had to apply far in advance and it is about a pound of paperwork.

The Moscow trip did require the visa even though it was offered by the cruise line. Also if you went to Moscow you did not have time to see any of the outstanding attractions in St. Petersburg. We decided it would be a mistake to miss St. Petersburg.

Our entire group did the same thing in St. Petersburg. We booked a shore excursion that consisted of two days of touring for ten hours each day. We were required to attend an orientation the night before we arrived in St. Petersburg. We were told the immigration people were very serious and they did not smile to anybody. Be professional when you present yourself and don't make wisecracks. Stay with your tour guide. Big brother is watching!

The two days in St. Petersburg were truly an exhausting experience. We were kept busy for ten hours each day but we saw some of Russia's most beautiful and historical attractions. Just to give you an idea, here are a few things we saw on our tours.

We had a few hours at the Hermitage Museum. That was just a taste because it is one of the largest in the world and you could spend days here and not see it all.

Catherine the I built one of the most ornate and beautiful palaces you can see anywhere. It was to be her summer home. The interior is heavily decorated with gold trims. The surrounding gardens are among the most beautiful in Russia. It is used now for major cultural and political events.

The Grand Palace at Peterhof was built by Peter the Great for summer vacations. It is said to be inspired after his visit to Versailles in France to compete with Louis the XIV. The grounds are large with numerous fountains and impeccably landscaped with ornate bushes and flowering plants. The property was enlarged several times especially by Elizabeth of Russia.

We had to clear immigration in and out of Russia each day of our two day tour. On the final day as we were leaving we presented our passports to a very stern faced official. I said to her in my very best Russian, "Vasvidaniya," and the biggest smile we'd seen in Russia appeared! So much for nobody smiles in Russia. Vasvidaniya in Russian means "goodbye", or literally, "until next meeting."

The next day we docked in Tallinn, Estonia. This small country is one of the most under rated ports of call. It has an old town and new town section. On our walk through the old town section we were surprised to see the Dalai Lama was in town. Security was high everywhere we went.

Gothenburg, even though it is Sweden's second largest city, was just a good place to walk around and enjoy shopping and having lunch in one of their outstanding restaurants. It was fun and a relaxing port of call after all the excitement of St. Petersburg and the long walking tours of Tallinn.

Mary and I had fears that our limo from the same company that was supposed to pick us up in London would not show up when we docked back in Harwich. I e-mailed back and forth with the company. They assured me they would have no issues with our return transfer from Harwich to Heathrow.

We called our group together to discuss options. It was guaranteed we could take Royal Caribbean's motor coaches to Heathrow airport without stress or problems. Or, we could take our chance with the other limo company. It was unanimous. We took the sure thing with Royal Caribbean.

Our transfer to Heathrow was without problems and our return flights were also without issue on Delta. What began with some bumps in the road turned out to be an excellent vacation enjoyed by everyone.

# Switzerland

Our flight from Chicago arrives in Geneva, Switzerland mid-morning after changing planes in Frankfurt. We cleared immigration and customs to the European Union in Frankfurt. In Geneva we meet our friend, Brad Dick who will be our tour guide for this trip in the baggage claim area. Brad is a highly professional tour guide and one of the best in the business. We've had him on other trips so we requested him for this trip from our tour operator.

We transferred to the Hotel Warwick. After lunch and check-in we met Brad for dinner including a few bottles of good wine. Brad uses this time to give an overview of the trip and the next day's itinerary.

Today we do a quick city tour of Geneva and move on to Montreux located at the foot of the beautiful Alps. This is a very pretty town and we had some time to walk around the lake area and take pictures.

In Switzerland it is necessary to use a local guide while visiting major cities. Of course, Brad arranges these in advance. We find our local guide and proceed on to Chillon Castle. This castle is a very photogenic castle and is one of the most visited castles in Switzerland as well as Europe. We spend a couple hours learning the history and visiting the inside and its dungeons. A very good stop.

We continue along the Rhone Valley to today's final destination, Zermatt. Access to the city of Zermatt was by train that we boarded in the city of Tasch. Zermatt is unique because they do not allow vehicles powered by gasoline engines. All the vehicles are battery powered. There are free shuttles taking guests where they want to go. We were told the reason is to prevent air pollution from harming the view of the Matterhorn. Even the police and emergency equipment is battery powered. Anyone wishing to operate a gas powered vehicle must apply for a special use permit. We're told they are very difficult to obtain!

Our hotel for the next two nights is the Hotel Alex. It is late afternoon when we arrive, just in time for their two for one happy hour. The group decided to eat outside at the hotel's restaurant. Not only was the food outstanding but we had a fantastic view of the Matterhorn as we dined!

We have viewed mountains on six continents but none are quite as impressive as the majestic Matterhorn. It is 14,692 feet high but is surrounded by at least four other mountains that are higher. What is so impressive is the solid rock formation jutting upward into the beautiful blue sky.

*The Matterhorn*

The highest cable car system in the world operates here in Zermatt. This ride was breath taking. The entire way to the top we have excellent views of the Matterhorn and of course everyone was taking pictures like crazy. Thank goodness for digital photography.

There is much to do at the top. Take an elevator down five stories beneath the glacier's ice ceiling. The Ice Palace is formed inside of a glacier. It is huge with many ice sculptures, and ice benches. The benches were covered with animal furs to make sitting comfortable. There were tunnels leading to toboggan runs and overlook areas with great views of the surrounding mountains.

This place would not be complete without the obligatory restaurant with some of the finest views in the world. I experienced the finest hot chocolate I believe I've ever had. Lunch was a very memorable experience with ceiling to floor glass windows with the view of the Matterhorn.

Since we are staying again this night in Zermatt, we are in no hurry to take the cable car back down. Zermatt is about the same altitude as Denver, Colorado but when you stand in the downtown and look to the Matterhorn you do not feel you're at that altitude.

After breakfast the next morning we board the electric vehicles and take them down to find our motor coach in the city of Tasch. This day is mostly sightseeing with several stops for photo ops before crossing into Italy for our Hotel Simplon Baveno on the shores of Lake Maggiore.

We had a late afternoon boat tour of Lake Maggiore where we stopped on a very large island called, Isola Bella. It is a privately owned island where the Borromeo family has a family home and floral gardens. Brad had arranged for us to go ashore and visit the home and gardens before we return to the hotel for dinner.

This trip was purposely constructed to give our group a great amount of traveling in the daytime to view beautiful scenic sites. We leave Lake Maggiore and ascend to Julier Pass, across the scenic Engadine Valley before arriving in St. Moritz.

St. Moritz is a very rich and cosmopolitan city. Some of the most expensive shopping in Switzerland is found in this city. The rich and famous jet setters find their way here. It scared me to hear we had the afternoon free for shopping. All turned out well, as nothing was purchased that would break the bank.

Brad had arranged an elegant dinner complete with good wine at our Hotel Crystal!

Today we leave St. Moritz and board the Glacier Express for our scenic train ride across the Grison Mountains through some unforgettable scenes of snow capped mountains and lush meadows. The coach is waiting for us in Chur and we reboard it for a scenic drive along the valley of the upper Rhine.

A stop in Vaduz the capital of Liechtenstein is quite interesting. Liechtenstein is the fourth smallest country in Europe, only sixty two square miles. It has borders with Switzerland and Austria. The city of Vaduz is sprinkled with picturesque steeple tops of the many churches and of course, the Gutenberg Castle. This was a very scenic and interesting stop. I was quite surprised that it is a member of the United Nations but is not a member of the European Union. They were, however, willing to accept our Euros for our purchases! It was fun to dine Al Fresco in the shadow of the Castle before making our way to Lucerne. We arrived in time for dinner on our own at a very small restaurant just a couple blocks from the Radisson Blu. The night was cool and we took an evening walk around the lake that was very scenic.

A local guide met us in Lucerne at our hotel the next morning. We had a very lengthy city tour that included a great amount of walking. When you travel don't under estimate the value of these city tours. These local guides are fountains of historical, business and local folk lore.

Our favorite area in Lucerne was the area surrounding the very famous Chapel Bridge. This wooden bridge is almost seven hundred feet long and our guide tells us it was constructed during the 14th century. When you see pictures of Switzerland on TV or in advertisements you will most likely see a picture of this bridge. There are small shops in the area and as you walk across the bridge several vendors have small areas to display trinkets you can purchase in memory of your trip to Lucerne and Switzerland.

We leave early after breakfast for Zurich because we have scheduled a very full day of sightseeing in Zurich. According to Brad, we will experience a long walking tour, a train, boat, tram and cable car rides.

Our local city guide meets us at a spot Brad had pre-arranged and boarded the bus. We drive a portion of Zurich where he gives us information about government and economy on the way to a train station.

Uetliberg Mountain top is 2,850 feet above sea level. We access it today by a short train trip from sea level to the summit. The train trip is about fifteen minutes to where we exit the train. It is still about another ten minute walk to the viewing point where we see the most beautiful panoramic view of Zurich. We're told how lucky we are because at this time of year many days the view is poor because of haze. Today is picture perfect and we take many photos before boarding the train for our return trip to the city level.

I think our guide is trying to impress us with exceptional views of the city. Next we're taken to the Polybahn cable car that takes us up to the Polyterrasse patio where we have more amazing views of Old Town, the lake and the city center.

When we return to the bottom on the cable car the local guide gives us all tickets for the tram and tells us to be sure to watch him because we are going to get off in the Old Town Area for a walking tour. The guide takes us through very narrow streets showing beautiful and elegant homes while giving us the history and business background of the city.

Our walking tour ends at the docking area where our group is to board a boat to take us around the Lake where we see the city from the perspective of the water.

We have a few minutes before the cruise. Brad told us Zurich is well known for making very good ice cream. There were many sidewalk vendors selling ice cream on the lake shore. Most of the group enjoyed a very nice treat before our cruise on Lake Zurich.

Circling the lake on the boat gave us a much different perspective about the city than what we had from our two views from above. It gave us a balanced overview and was a fitting ending of our tour of Zurich.

We ended our trip to Switzerland with a celebration dinner and wine at the hotel. Brad had been outstanding once again. Everyone assured him they would see him again on another trip in the future.

As our flight left Zurich we watched from our window as the beautiful mountain scenery was left behind for the next group of tourists to enjoy.

# Antarctica

Most people that travel often usually have the goal of traveling on all seven continents. Antarctica is usually the most difficult continent for them to visit. We had clients that were very interested in this trip. We felt in order to see several parts of Antarctica we should do a cruise.

After much research we decided on a cruise line that seemed like it had a very good itinerary. We sent invitations to fifty of our top clients and invited them to a dinner where we would show a video and have a representative make a presentation.

Interest was great and the room was full. Projectors were in place and our man was prepared and ready. I asked him one question. "How many times do we actually set foot on the continent?" It was just ten minutes before we were to begin the program but he said, "I don't know, let me make a phone call."

Mary and I were ready to begin when he motioned for us to come to the hallway. He told us, "You don't get to step on the land you just sail by and see the scenery." We told him that was a game changer. Nobody in the room would go if they could not actually get onto the continent itself. He was very nice and said he would make his presentation anyway since he and our clients were already here.

We were honest with everyone and told them what we had found out just minutes before. The cruise representative did a very good presentation but left knowing he would not be getting our business.

After much more research we decided on an expedition cruise offered by Hurtigruten Cruise Lines based in Norway. They have been cruising Antarctica for over a hundred twenty five years. They know the rules and are the top rated expedition explorer to Antarctica.

Antarctica has very strict laws about how to visit the continent. No ship that holds more than five hundred passengers can actually allow passengers on the continent. That was the reason our first choice could not allow passengers on land. Their ship far exceeded five hundred passengers.

Mary and I soon found out, this was no ordinary group. Hurtigruten had rules we had never encountered. If we as representatives of our clients missed any detail, our people could be denied boarding.

First, every person had to fill out a five page medical history form and carry it with them and present it in order to board the ship. Next, each person must have a Doctor's form stating the Doctor felt the person was in good health and was physically able to make a trip of this intensity. The form from the Doctor must be signed less than thirty days prior to boarding the ship. Finally, every person must purchase or provide evidence of travel insurance.

There were very strict passport requirements and we required every person to provide copies to us. We carried copies of everyone's passport with us just in case of loss or issues. This is something we usually require when traveling to exotic destinations or where there are strict visa or passport requirements.

We had never been to Buenos Aires before and Mary felt we should go a couple days before we were to meet the cruise people. She is one of the best in the business at finding the best things to do when we go early like this. She out did herself in Buenos Aires!

Most of our group flew from Moline to Dallas on the 1 P.M. flight on February 19th. Our flight to Buenos Aires did not leave until 9:20 P.M. This was an overnight flight arriving about 10 A.M. their local time. One couple had flown from Miami and had arrived a couple hours before we did. They would meet us when we had cleared immigration and customs.

I had spent a great deal of time finding a company to transfer the group from the airport to the Hotel Inter Continental Santiago because no matter what, the cruise line would not transfer our group and they would not give us any information as to who to contact for that service. The only way they would transfer us would be if we arrived on the day the trip was to begin.

Our flight landed on time. All of us on that flight went into the same line at passport control. We were almost two hours in the passport line! Since we were in the immigration area no cell phones could be used! It clearly said phones would be confiscated if you tried to use them. Our friends knew our flight had landed and so did the transfer company. Both were very concerned when we did not clear customs in a reasonable time.

I had to laugh when we cleared customs and entered the general population because there was Lynda holding a sign saying Fislar group! She and Gary had seen the transfer company person with our sign and introduced themselves to them. They were very helpful in keeping the transfer people from leaving.

As I mentioned Mary had found a Dinner and Tango show that night. Just FYI, don't go to Buenos Aires and fail to see a Dinner and Tango show! She had researched the numerous companies that advertised for shows like that. She found a company that had very good reviews and had been performing for a great many years. Since we had enough people they would pick us up at the hotel and return us after the show.

We were seated at a front row table by the stage. Again, great work Mary! Usually when we travel steak just does not compare to the steaks we have here in the States. We had choices of New York Strip, pasta, chicken, or a vegan meal. Anything we wanted to drink was also included.

I had heard Argentina wine and beef were among the best in the world. Our New York Strips were some of the best steaks we've had anywhere including the States. The wine kept coming. If your glass was half empty they were there to fill it. Absolutely everything about this evening was perfect.

They picked us up exactly as they said, the show was extremely well produced, and we had the best table in the house, the steaks were outstanding and of course we had lots of really good Argentina wine.

Mary earned another gold star the next day. She had arranged a full day fiesta at a Gaucho Ranch!

To many of our friends, a trip to a Gaucho Ranch was truly a new experience. Many of them were, "city folks" and did not have much experience with farms, much less, a Gaucho Ranch.

Mary had found a tour to the Santa Susana Ranch that would pick up the group at our hotel. We were picked up between 8 and 8:30 A.M. Buenos Aires is a very large metropolitan area with major traffic issues. Not having to work with a separate transfer company was a real benefit. It turned out to be quite a distance to the ranch. We were also familiar with the tour company, Viator. We had used this company in other parts of the world and their service was always very good. This tour was highly rated by clients of Viator.

Upon arrival at the ranch we were greeted by women in colorful authentic dresses and piping hot empanadas and a choice of either red or white Argentina wines. Empanadas are pastry crusts filled with either beef or chicken. They can also be provided as a vegan treat.

A real treat of the day was to be the horseback ride. Having lived on farms as a youngster I had ridden often. Mary and her sister had only one experience with horses. They were a little worried. There was an option to ride in a carriage if the horses did not suit you. The girls did decide to ride with the group on the horses. All went very well and we all had a great ride.

*Mary at Santa Susana Ranch*

They have a Spanish-colonial house on the grounds that is a museum and was interesting to visit while we awaited our parrillada. This was an Argentine style BBQ that included beef, pork and chicken done on a twenty foot long grill. While we ate, folk singers and Tango dancers entertained.

After lunch we watched the Gauchos provide an exciting show of expert horsemanship skills before we had to board our motor coach back to our hotel. This turned out to be an excellent tour. Everyone had a really good time today!

We returned to our hotel around 5:30 P.M. just in time to check in with our Hurtigruten people to complete our arrangements for tomorrow's flight and the cruise.

Hurtigruten transferred us to the smaller airport in Buenos Aires for our three hour charter flight to Ushuaia, Argentina. Ushuaia has the distinction of being the most southern city on the planet. There are no full time residents on Antarctica. There are only research outposts. Ushuaia is located 680 nautical miles north of Antarctica.

After a short city tour of Ushuaia, we were dropped off downtown Ushuaia for some shopping prior to boarding the MS *MIDNATSOL*.

Directly after boarding the ship at 3 P.M., we were checked by a medical team to be certain we had the necessary medical forms from our Doctor and did not have a temperature. We were then given a scheduled time for us to pick up boots that are loaned to everyone for this trip for use free of charge and to pick up the complimentary expedition jacket everyone must wear for the landings. This jacket is wind and water resistant and is a bright orange color for safety. The jacket is ours to keep.

We entered the Drake Passage a few hours after we departed Ushuaia. Each hour the seas became a little rougher. Announcements were made telling everyone tonight we would be cruising through some of the roughest waters in the world. The Captain advised everyone to go to their cabin after dinner and secure everything in it to keep things from moving about. He suggested everyone ride out the rough seas in bed.

Several in this group had been on the *Viking Sky* and had been helicoptered off that ship in a hurricane just a few months before. Needless to say we had some anxiety when seas really became seriously rough.

Mary and I did a thorough check of the cabin and felt we had secured it well. In the middle of the night it was all we could do to stay safely in our beds. Small items began to bounce around and break! We are at sea the next day and slowly the seas began to calm.

We had been assigned to landing groups. Our group was called "Chinstraps." Each day when we were at our destinations, we would do a landing and a cruising. Times were assigned randomly with some landing in the morning with cruising in the afternoon. Other times the cruising and landing could be reversed. Cruising in the Zodiacs allowed us to get very close to the icebergs, whales, penguins and other wildlife in the sea.

The landing boats were called Zodiacs. They were large rubber boats holding about twelve to fourteen people plus the driver. Twin 150 HP engines powered the Zodiacs. The Zodiac had two hard rubber hulls. Because we would be cruising through water with large chunks of ice, the double hulls were a safety measure in case the outer layer would be torn by jagged ice pieces.

On Monday, February 24th we arrived at our first stop in Antarctica, Deception Island and we did our first landing in Antarctica. It is a part of the South Shetland Islands and used to be a whaling station. The whaling station is now abandoned. The weather was good and the temperature was a balmy thirty-seven degrees.

Deception Island is home to large colonies of chinstrap penguins and is noted for its warm volcanic soil. If you dig down in the sand on the beach you will find very hot water. The volcanic soil warms the water close to shore and many passengers, including one of our group, came dressed in their bathing suits and went for a swim! They earned a certificate proclaiming they swam in Antarctica. Mary and I were content to watch, no swimming for us!

We arrived at Danco Island early the next day. This is actually one of only two places where we will actually walk on the continent itself. The morning was spent in the Zodiac boat cruising the shoreline. There were numerous sightings of whales, seals and penguins. Our landing in the afternoon was excellent. The temp today was thirty-four degrees when we departed the ship. On shore we saw large colonies of penguins. Even though we saw a great many we were told other places would have considerably more.

Our stop at the Gonzales Videla research station was rich with wildlife. On our Zodiac cruise we saw a number of whales up close and one whale came out of the water very close to one of the Zodiacs. Quite a sight to see. When we did our landing it was almost impossible to walk the path to the research station because there were so many penguins in the way. There were literally thousands of them as far as you could see. Of course, when there are that many penguins there is also quite a smell. We could smell the island before our ship was even close to it.

The visit to Petermann Island was the most treacherous landing we had. Our Zodiacs pushed against giant rocks and was held firm with the engines and crew members. Crew members would assist us over the rocks until we arrived at the land area. The biggest reason for landing here was for the view as we walked to the top of the hills. When you reached the top, the mountains and the icebergs in the water were a picture worth seeing. However boarding the Zodiacs for the return was a dangerous experience. This day was our warmest of the trip. It topped out at forty degrees.

Our next to last stop was Charlotte Bay and Portal Point. The weather had turned cold. Thirty degrees and snow. The cruising in the Zodiacs was very uncomfortable and we were thankful for our wind and waterproof jackets that had been provided by Hurtigruten. This was also the second time we were able to step on the continent proper.

Every time we cruised on the Zodiacs we would see amazing iceberg formations. Many were larger than our ship, others much smaller. Many were colored in beautiful shades of blue and green. Our Zodiac guide told us the older icebergs are usually the ones with the pretty colors. The refraction of light also will create unusual colors in icebergs. Icebergs in this area are usually much older and we were treated to many very beautiful and shapely ones this day.

***Dick & Mary in Antarctica***

Our final landing is to be on Ronge Island. We had a scheduled landing at 11:40 A.M. and the final cruising in the Zodiac at 4:05 P.M. Mary and I did not miss a single landing or cruising. Some of the passengers found the vigorous schedule to be far too demanding. By this time many were content to stay on board and rest.

Expedition cruises are very different from what most people expect, or have experienced in the Caribbean. There are times set aside each day for lectures covering many subjects relevant to the upcoming adventures for that particular cruise.

Hurtigruten is exceptionally skilled at booking highly educated experts on their Expedition cruises. We tried to attend each lecture. People that missed the lectures missed a great amount they needed to know to get the most out of this amazing cruise.

Upon leaving Ronge Island we would travel two more days at sea and would again cross the Drake Passage. We did a much better job of securing the loose items in the cabin this time.

The MS *MIDNATSOL* was equipped with satellite TV and a very erratic internet. During our two days at sea, March 2 and 3 we began hearing about a virus that might turn into a pandemic. Flights in and out of Buenos Aires were being canceled and we began to worry about being able to return home.

We disembarked in Ushuaia about 8:30 A.M. and had a couple free hours for last-minute shopping before we were transferred to the airport for our charter flight to the small airport in Buenos Aires. Hurtigruten would not transfer from the charter airport to the International airport on the same day you disembark. They highly recommend an overnight stay again before flying home.

Our group wanted to return the same day and I had the same company transfer us between airports we had used when we arrived. It was an easy transfer. However, from the time we left the MS *MIDNATSOL* until we arrived home was a journey of 10,000 miles and thirty three hours!

It was only a few days after we returned that the Pandemic was declared and international travel became very difficult. We learned the passengers that traveled on the MS *MIDNATSOL* on the very next cruise were delayed over a week returning to the States.

Antarctica was one of the most physically demanding trips because of the distance and the rugged areas we visited. The Hurtigruten crew, expedition members, and of course kitchen staff were outstanding. It is one of the most interesting trips we have experienced.

# Chasing the Northern Lights

The Northern Lights can be seen sometimes in the Midwest areas of Illinois and Iowa. This does not happen often and from all we've been told they can be spectacular viewing.

We found a cruise departing from Bergen, Norway, on March 14th sailing north above the Arctic Circle with ports of call along the Western coast of Norway then back South along the same coast with the last Norwegian port being Stavanger. After Stavanger we would have a restful day at sea before disembarking in London after twelve days and nights aboard the *Viking Sky*.

The attraction to most of our friends was the opportunity to possibly see fantastic displays of the Northern Lights. Our group consisted of fifteen people that have traveled with us many times to several exotic destinations.

Some of us, my sister-in-law Marcy and our good friends, Gary and Lynda, and Ed and Bev joined Mary and me to fly into Bergen a couple days before the cruise was to depart. We had excellent accommodations at the Raddison Blu Hotel situated downtown on the ocean front and actually close enough to walk to the pier when it became time to board the ship.

Our first day in Bergen was mostly transferring from the airport to the hotel, getting checked in and taking a hop on hop off tour of Bergen. We all met for a light dinner and turned out the lights early for a good night's rest.

The concierge mentioned we should not miss the view of the city from the top of Mount Ulriken. All of us walked to the cable car for a scenic ride to the top. We had a really good lunch at the restaurant on top and then enjoyed a most impressive view of the city and the bay.

Much to our surprise just as we arrived at the lookout point, our ship, the *Viking Sky* was just entering the harbor. It was a beautiful and impressive sight and we were excited because we would be boarding this beautiful ship the next day.

*Marcy, Lynda, Gary, Mary, Dick*
*The Viking Sky is arriving in the background*

We slept later the next morning, had breakfast and at the appropriate time we walked with our luggage to the pier and boarded the beautiful *Viking Sky*. The ship remained overnight in Bergen and they provided another city tour for us.

The next day we sailed Norway's Inside Passage. Spectacular scenery! We visited the port of Narvik where we enjoyed a city tour. Then we sailed to the port of Alta where the ship docked overnight. This was so we could take a late-night tour inland away from the lights with the hope of seeing a brilliant display of the Northern Lights.

It was worth the long drive each way and the late-night hours. Although the lights were not as bright as we hoped there were several times where we did see a nice display.

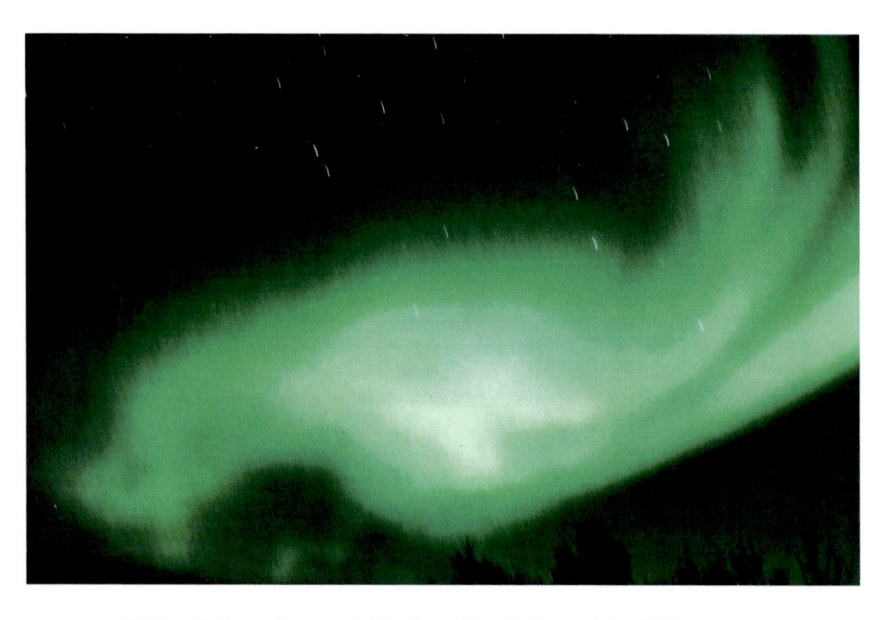

**The Northern Lights In Narvik, Norway**

Our next port of call was Tromso, Norway. Here too, we did overnight in port on the ship. Upon arrival most of our group spent a great amount of time shopping away the daylight hours. We were treated with a light snowfall in Tromso making the city a beautiful picture. A highlight of the trip was an evening organ concert in the Arctic Cathedral. The Cathedral was small but the music, lighting and atmosphere were quite beautiful and memorable.

We sailed from Tromso the next morning heading to the port of Bodo. Later that afternoon the Captain said we would not stop in the Bodo port because high winds made it dangerous to enter through a narrow entrance to the harbor. We did feel a little more movement aboard the ship the rest of that day and through the night.

The next morning, after breakfast, Gary, Lynda, Marcy, Mary and I met to play trivia in the Explorer's Lounge on deck eight about 10:00 A.M. This lasted for about an hour. The ship was experiencing considerable movement and through the front windows of the lounge we could see waves crashing against the windows even though we were on deck eight, the top deck of the ship.

After the trivia was over Marcy, Mary and I decided we would go and see what we could find for lunch. As we exited the Explorer Lounge we met up with one of the ship's lecture people. When you take exotic trips like this usually the cruise line or tour operator will provide very good guest lecturers.

Mike Dispezio was one of the best on board and we had developed a good relationship with him and his wife Susan.

We chatted briefly and he mentioned, according to weather reports we would be encountering sixty to sixty-five knot winds later in the afternoon. Being a former pilot and familiar with converting knots to miles per hour I said to everyone. "That's seventy five to eighty miles per hour winds!"

Winds that high are almost, if not, hurricane force and are extremely dangerous to ships in the open ocean. It was obvious it was going to be a rough ride until we were able to sail through the storm.

Marcy, Mary and I went to lunch on deck seven by the pool at the Wintergarden snack bar. The ship was rocking so violently the water was splashing out of the pool. We took seats far away but the lunch was excellent. I remember a corned beef sandwich and a very tasty rhubarb dessert.

The three of us enjoyed lunch and Mary said at 1:00 P.M. the movie showing in the theater on deck two would be, *The Green Book*. We'd heard good things about this movie and thought it would be a good way to pass some hours while we sailed through the rough seas.

About half way through the movie, about 1:45 P.M. the movie stopped. The projectionist came out and asked if anyone could tell him where it was in the movie when it stopped so he could restart it. However the ship continued to violently shake and roll. We could hear heavy equipment backstage moving side to side. The equipment was crashing about and quite noisy as it bashed about backstage. The movie did not start again.

Furniture on cruise ships is usually very heavy in order to keep it from moving in the event of rough seas. Marcy was sitting on a couch that went from aisle to aisle and it was bolted to the floor. Mary and I were sitting on chairs that were so heavy it was difficult to move them.

A wave struck the ship with such violence that Mary and I were thrown ten to twelve feet with the chairs on top of us! Within a minute the Captain announced,

"This is not a drill, this is a real emergency. Go to your muster stations."

The theater was Marcy's muster station. Mary and my muster station was at the other end of the ship in the restaurant. We decided since we are family we would stay where we were and not separate.

Very shortly the crew began passing out life jackets. That process took about an hour. As the crew was doing this the Captain announced we had lost power in all four engines. We were adrift in the ocean without power. He also advised he had issued a Mayday call for assistance. The emergency lighting activated so we did have light.

The Captain made regular updates on our situation. This happened about every thirty minutes. Soon, he advised they were able to restore power in one engine but that was not enough to restore stability to the ship or try to sail. He advised he had dropped the anchor and it had stopped the ship from drifting.

The ship continued violent movement up and down and side to side. It was almost impossible to walk. The Captain advised the Norwegian National Guard was sending helicopters to take people off the ship as a result of his Mayday call. He said they had about four or five that would be evacuating everyone. He also said this would be a long process due to the very foul weather. Priority would be given to passengers injured and those violently sick from the ship's movement for the evacuation process.

Mary realized we did not have hats, coats or gloves and even if we were lucky to be chosen for evacuation we would have serious problems in this cold winter storm. I volunteered to try to get to our cabin and get what I could.

As I left the theater, our friends Gary and Lynda were just entering. Gary was covered to his waist with blood from a serious cut on his head. Both he and Lynda were soaking wet. Neither had a dry stitch on them. They were being helped by crew members. I showed them where we were sitting and asked the crew members to take them to us.

It took a while but I got our coats, hats and gloves and returned to the theater. The crew brought Gary and Lynda blankets and told them, modesty was not an issue, they needed to remove their cold wet clothing. The crew went to their cabin and brought dry clothing for both of them.

When they were taken care of, we were anxious to know what had happened to them. As it turned out, they were in the restaurant muster station where Mary and I should have been. A huge wave hit the large glass windows where they were sitting and broke the windows! It flooded the area and swept them across the room under water, tables, chairs and other people. Certainly they did not feel they would survive!

We were concerned about everyone in our group. We could only account for nine of them in the theater. There was no way to know where or what happened to the other six.

The crew was doing all they possibly could. They were tending to the many injured passengers. By this time we had been in the muster station for several hours. The crew passed through bringing what food they could find. Of course it was not much. Mary and I split a bag of potato chips. Later some cucumber finger sandwiches came. Many were so sea sick eating was out of the question. There were hundreds of people and a small tray of brownies did not go very far.

With the Captain making regular announcements, passing out small amounts of food by the crew and assurance that helicopters would be taking passengers off soon, the atmosphere remained calm. Although, when a passenger began singing, "Swing Low Sweet Chariot" it caused some concern. I believe they were asked to sing quietly or just to themselves so that people would not panic.

Things turned worse when the bathrooms on our deck ceased to work. It soon became an unbelievable mess and they had to lock the doors to the bathrooms. Finally they announced crew members would take people in groups of three to higher decks for use of bathrooms. That did seem to work.

We realized we did not have our passports or Mary's medicine. If or when we were to be taken off the ship by helicopter, we would have several issues trying to travel back home without them. On a bathroom trip Mary with the help of a crew member was able to make it to our cabin to retrieve the passports.

It should be noted here that our cabin was a terrible mess when she entered. There was broken glass scattered over the floor. Any bottles, glasses or anything breakable was broken. The bathroom was the same but Mary's medicine in a plastic bottle was fine. She was able to find her medicine and the passports and return to the theater.

The crew was taking the injured people from the theater and restaurant muster stations to deck eight for treatments and evacuations. It was almost midnight when our friends, Gary and Lynda were moved to deck eight for evacuation. We had been in life jackets and the muster station for almost eleven hours!

About this time the Captain announced a second engine was operational but it was still not enough power to try and sail. Helicopters would continue to remove passengers.

Four or five helicopters were working on removing people from our ship. They could only load one at a time and it was a half-hour flight from the ship to where they could unload and another half-hour trip back to the ship. It was a long process just to take twenty passengers off. We had 930 passengers on board plus the crew members.

The Captain announced that evacuation would be slowed because a cargo ship very close to us was also in trouble and a couple of our helicopters were going to try and assist that ship. We learned later that they had a crew of nine on the cargo ship. They put on thermal suits and jumped into the ocean. Their ship sunk but our helicopters were able to rescue all nine of them.

It was almost 3:00 A.M. and a crew member quietly asked a couple seated next to me if they wanted to evacuate. It was a voluntary decision as to whether you wanted to take the helicopter or not. They said, "no."

Earlier the three of us had discussed what we would do. We decided that if offered it would be a quick answer, "Yes." I quietly told the crew member the three of us wanted to go. He said, "Okay, let's go." We were assisted up the stairs from deck two to deck eight and put into a queue for the helicopter.

We were kept inside until it was our turn to be taken off. I believe it was for two reasons. First, the weather outside was dreadful. Second, if we were to see what happened as others were lifted off, we might change our minds.

It was our turn! The ship was still tossing violently. When we stepped outside on deck eight we saw the helicopter several hundred feet above the ship and the ocean! Mary had her purse with her but they told her the ride would be so rough she would not be able to hang onto it and it would fall into the ocean. She explained it had our passports and her medicine and we needed it badly. The helicopter crew member that was hooking people up took the purse but said he would be the last person to come up on the flight and he would bring it up with him.

The crew member asked us to face each other. A small cable was put behind each of our backs and brought forward under our armpits. Both ends hooked together and to each other. Then we were attached to the long cable that dangled from the helicopter.

I told Mary, "Don't look down, just look up." The crew member asked, "Are you ready?" We both looked at each other and said, "YES!"

Instantly we were lifted off the ship out over the ocean. The wind was howling. It was dark and we were spinning like a top with rain, sleet and snow hitting our faces. When we reached the opening of the helicopter two men were there. One grabbed me and the other grabbed Mary and pulled us aboard. After they removed the cables from us we were shoved to a sitting position on the floor.

Marcy came up on the next lift with another person. The crew member from below came next with Mary's purse! We looked around and were surprised to see there were almost twenty others already on board.

The doors were closed and we're on our way to safety off the ship to a small National Guard facility that was about a twenty-five to thirty minute flight.

When we touched down and the helicopter doors opened we slid on our bottoms to the opening. A Norwegian National Guard member took hold of us by each arm and walked us to to the facility.

At three different locations we had to give our name, birth date and cabin number. We were offered toothpaste, tooth brush, clean socks and underwear if necessary. A nurse checked us out to be sure we were medically okay and then we boarded a bus to a hotel in Molde, Norway.

We arrived at the hotel and we were promptly checked into our room. We had been awake now for almost thirty hours under very stressful conditions and we needed a shower and sleep. Not so, Viking passengers needed to meet in two hours.

When we finally got to the room we turned on the television. Every channel was showing our ship and reporting on the situation. By this time it was daylight. A news helicopter was showing pictures of the ship. It was anchored only about a hundred feet from huge rocks and listing at about a thirty-degree angle! Had the Captain not dropped the anchor, or if the anchor would not have held, we would have certainly crashed into the rocks and the ship would have sunk with everyone on board.

Seeing the pictures on television made us realize the severity of our situation. The rescue helicopters were still evacuating passengers. At this point, we had no idea where our other clients and friends were or what had happened to them. We were told passengers were taken to at least four hotels in different cities.

The meeting did not last long. We were each given money to purchase food, clothes or whatever we needed. Viking Cruise Lines arranged dinner that evening for all of us and told us the next morning the Chairman of the Board of Viking would meet with us.

When morning arrived, the skies had cleared. Chairman Torstein Hagen met with all of us. He advised all resources of Viking Cruise Lines was at work to get all passengers new airline reservations back to their home cities. Desks were set up in each hotel to assist us. When we got ours, Mary's sister Marcy was not on the same flights. We worked with the air desk and were able to get our reservations together.

Tug boats had been attached to the *Viking Sky* and it was being towed to Molde and should arrive late afternoon. Later we were told we would be bused to the ship around 6:00 P.M. and we would have forty-five minutes to pack all our belongings and then be dropped at the Molde airport.

It was almost impossible to comprehend when we got to our room. The room had been cleaned and straightened. It was as if nothing had happened. We packed and took the bus to the Molde airport.

Our itinerary was to fly from Molde to Oslo and have a layover of several hours. Then we would fly to Stockholm, Sweden and then direct to Chicago.

That sounded simple and they were going to bus us to a hotel in Oslo then back to the airport for our Stockholm flight.

With all the busing involved we figured we'd have only about an hour and a half in the hotel. We slept on the floor of the Oslo airport before boarding our flight to Stockholm. Those flights were routine flights.

I know this has been a long chapter. There is no way the written word can accurately describe the seriousness of this ordeal or capture the emotion and stress involved. I suggest you go to www.youtube.com and search "Viking Sky Cruise Ship". There are about six or eight videos that accurately show the severity of our situation.

We've been asked, "Will you ever cruise again." The answer is, we will and we have cruised. Cruising remains one of the safest and most interesting ways to travel. Perhaps we'll see you on board sometime. Just look for the couple called, Dick & Mary.

# About the Author

Dick and Mary Fislar have owned a travel agency for over thirty years. They specialize in hosting groups to the world's most interesting destinations. Their travel agency belongs to Mast Vacation Partners, a highly respected Midwest travel consortium. Dick enjoys many interests that have helped in the travel business. He has a pilot's license, a Managing Broker Real Estate license, a degree in business administration and a CPM certification, and years of experience in the world of finance.

Dick and Mary are avid runners and both have been inducted into the Hall of Fame for runners in the Quad Cities. They take the opportunity to run together as they travel around the world.